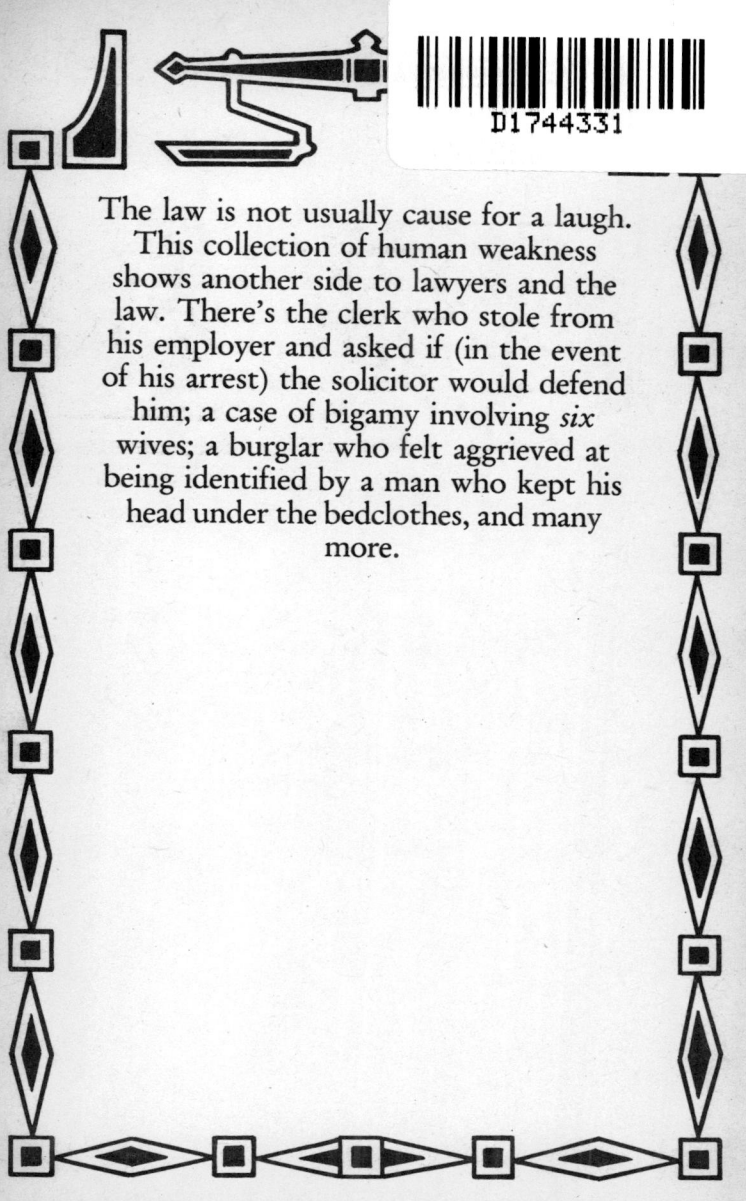

The law is not usually cause for a laugh. This collection of human weakness shows another side to lawyers and the law. There's the clerk who stole from his employer and asked if (in the event of his arrest) the solicitor would defend him; a case of bigamy involving *six* wives; a burglar who felt aggrieved at being identified by a man who kept his head under the bedclothes, and many more.

Trial & Error

Or,
Beyond the Legal Limit!

Compiled by

Richard De'ath

London
UNWIN PAPERBACKS
Boston   Sydney

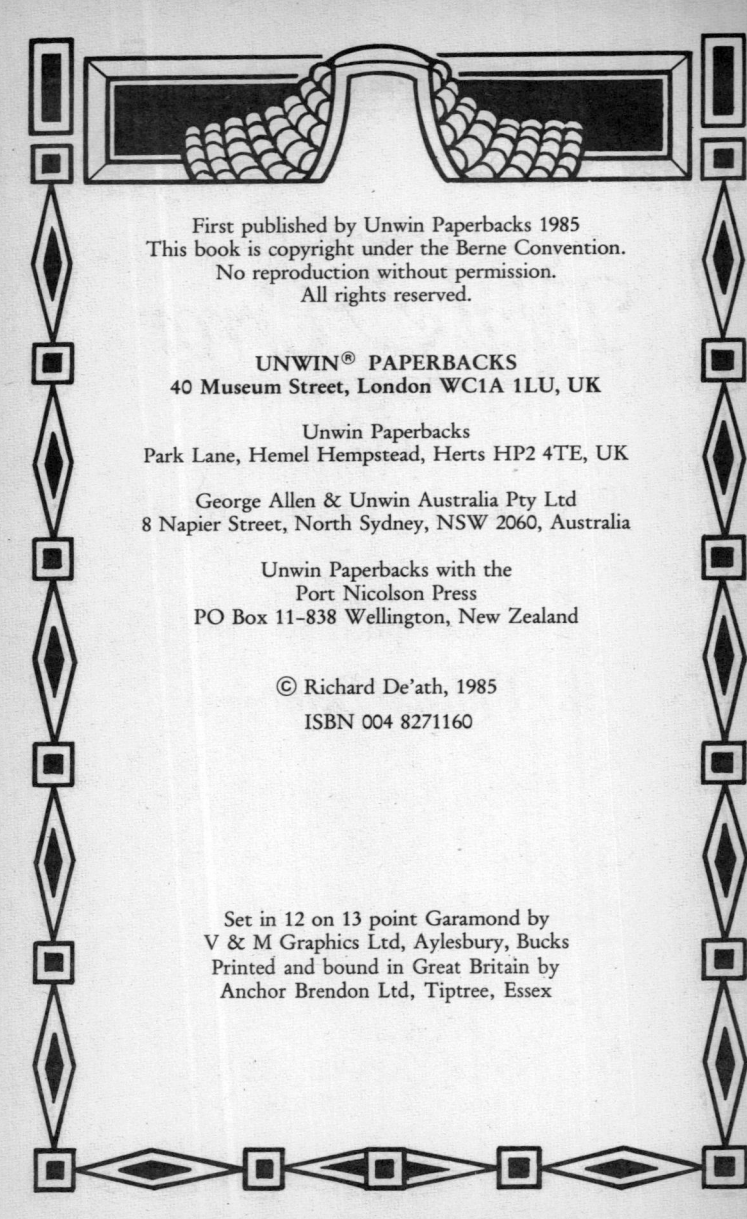

First published by Unwin Paperbacks 1985

UNWIN® PAPERBACKS
40 Museum Street, London WC1A 1LU, UK

Unwin Paperbacks
Park Lane, Hemel Hempstead, Herts HP2 4TE, UK

George Allen & Unwin Australia Pty Ltd
8 Napier Street, North Sydney, NSW 2060, Australia

Unwin Paperbacks with the
Port Nicolson Press
PO Box 11–838 Wellington, New Zealand

© Richard De'ath, 1985

ISBN 004 8271160

Set in 12 on 13 point Garamond by
V & M Graphics Ltd, Aylesbury, Bucks
Printed and bound in Great Britain by
Anchor Brendon Ltd, Tiptree, Essex

CONTENTS

For

JOHN MORTIMER

– a little brief humour

PREFACE

A few years ago a policeman was being cross-examined in a case of drunkenness. Asked by counsel to describe what the defendant was doing at the time of his arrest, the constable replied, 'He was having a very heated argument with a taxi driver.'

'But *that* doesn't prove he was drunk,' retorted the counsel, hitching up his gown on to his shoulders in a gesture of triumph.

'No,' replied the policeman evenly, 'but there wasn't a taxi driver there!'

The very idea of the austere courtroom, the dark-gowned officials of the law, and the trials and tribulations of humanity which are paraded there, would seem to be anything but conducive to humour. Yet, of course, as all human life is there, and the dividing line between joy and sorrow can be so narrow, closer examination soon reveals that laughter, both intentional and unintentional, has a habit of getting into the proceedings.

As the legal authority, J. A. R. Cairns, put it most precisely in his book, *The Loom of the Law*:

Like life itself, it is packed with paradoxes, incongruities, absurdities, laughter jostles the heels of despair, sunshine peeps through clouds and shadows, yet everything seems just as it ought to be. The loom has been built piece by

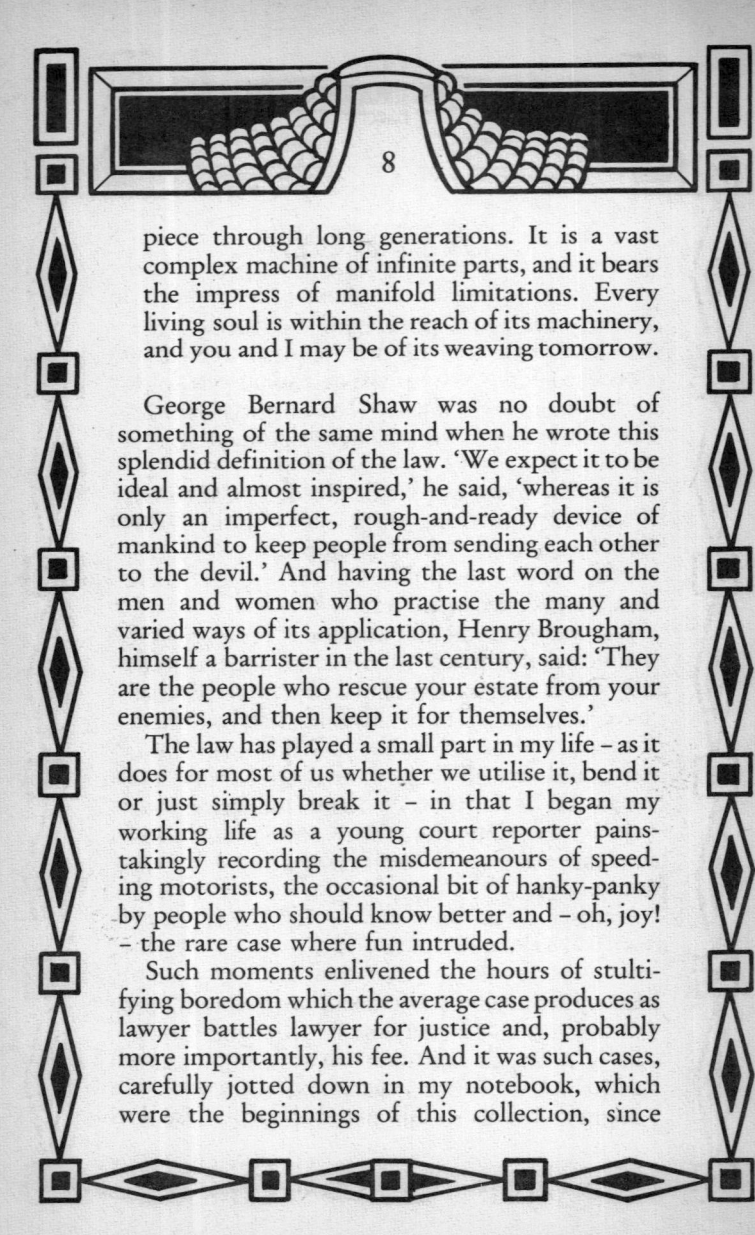

piece through long generations. It is a vast complex machine of infinite parts, and it bears the impress of manifold limitations. Every living soul is within the reach of its machinery, and you and I may be of its weaving tomorrow.

George Bernard Shaw was no doubt of something of the same mind when he wrote this splendid definition of the law. 'We expect it to be ideal and almost inspired,' he said, 'whereas it is only an imperfect, rough-and-ready device of mankind to keep people from sending each other to the devil.' And having the last word on the men and women who practise the many and varied ways of its application, Henry Brougham, himself a barrister in the last century, said: 'They are the people who rescue your estate from your enemies, and then keep it for themselves.'

The law has played a small part in my life – as it does for most of us whether we utilise it, bend it or just simply break it – in that I began my working life as a young court reporter painstakingly recording the misdemeanours of speeding motorists, the occasional bit of hanky-panky by people who should know better and – oh, joy! – the rare case where fun intruded.

Such moments enlivened the hours of stultifying boredom which the average case produces as lawyer battles lawyer for justice and, probably more importantly, his fee. And it was such cases, carefully jotted down in my notebook, which were the beginnings of this collection, since

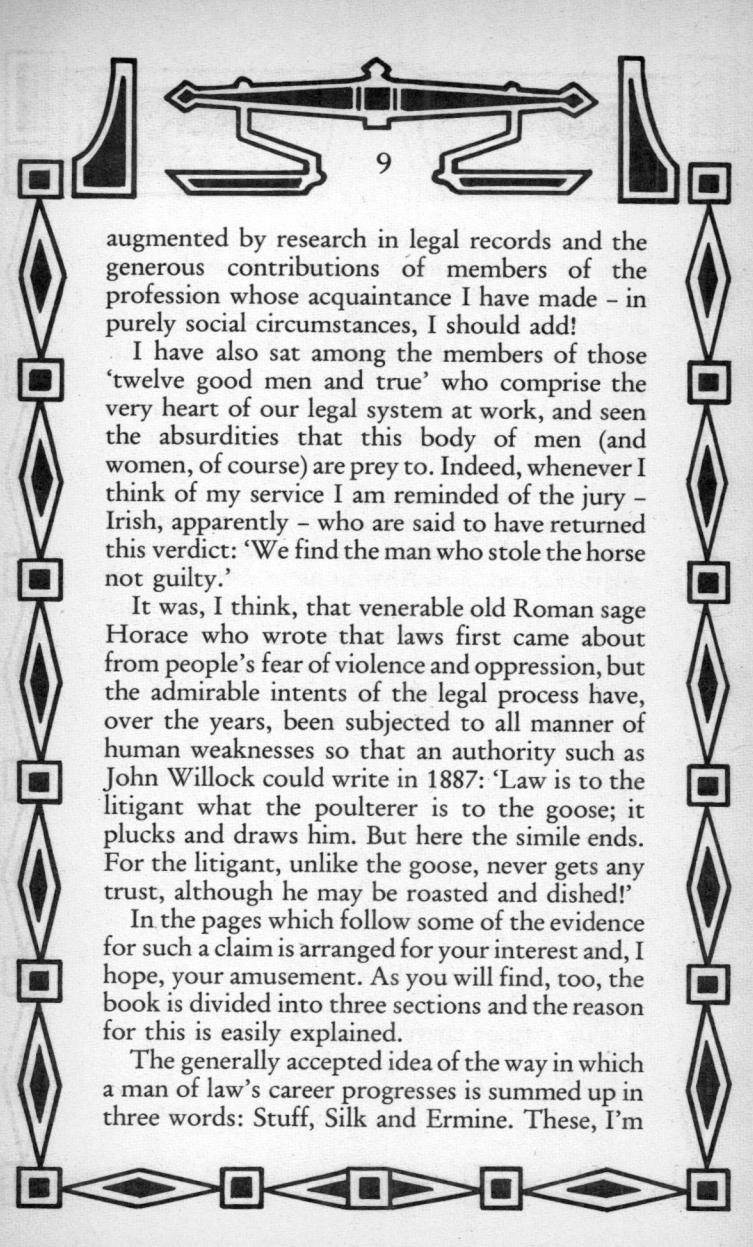

augmented by research in legal records and the generous contributions of members of the profession whose acquaintance I have made – in purely social circumstances, I should add!

I have also sat among the members of those 'twelve good men and true' who comprise the very heart of our legal system at work, and seen the absurdities that this body of men (and women, of course) are prey to. Indeed, whenever I think of my service I am reminded of the jury – Irish, apparently – who are said to have returned this verdict: 'We find the man who stole the horse not guilty.'

It was, I think, that venerable old Roman sage Horace who wrote that laws first came about from people's fear of violence and oppression, but the admirable intents of the legal process have, over the years, been subjected to all manner of human weaknesses so that an authority such as John Willock could write in 1887: 'Law is to the litigant what the poulterer is to the goose; it plucks and draws him. But here the simile ends. For the litigant, unlike the goose, never gets any trust, although he may be roasted and dished!'

In the pages which follow some of the evidence for such a claim is arranged for your interest and, I hope, your amusement. As you will find, too, the book is divided into three sections and the reason for this is easily explained.

The generally accepted idea of the way in which a man of law's career progresses is summed up in three words: Stuff, Silk and Ermine. These, I'm

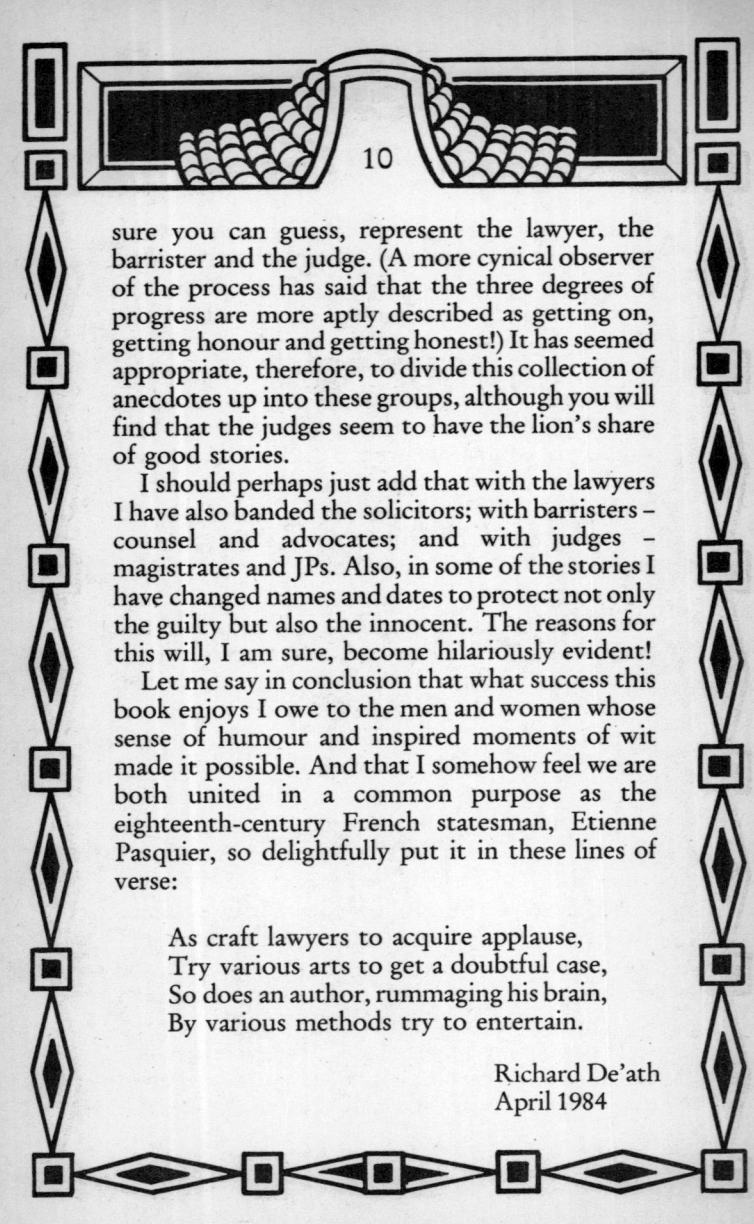

sure you can guess, represent the lawyer, the barrister and the judge. (A more cynical observer of the process has said that the three degrees of progress are more aptly described as getting on, getting honour and getting honest!) It has seemed appropriate, therefore, to divide this collection of anecdotes up into these groups, although you will find that the judges seem to have the lion's share of good stories.

I should perhaps just add that with the lawyers I have also banded the solicitors; with barristers – counsel and advocates; and with judges – magistrates and JPs. Also, in some of the stories I have changed names and dates to protect not only the guilty but also the innocent. The reasons for this will, I am sure, become hilariously evident!

Let me say in conclusion that what success this book enjoys I owe to the men and women whose sense of humour and inspired moments of wit made it possible. And that I somehow feel we are both united in a common purpose as the eighteenth-century French statesman, Etienne Pasquier, so delightfully put it in these lines of verse:

As craft lawyers to acquire applause,
Try various arts to get a doubtful case,
So does an author, rummaging his brain,
By various methods try to entertain.

Richard De'ath
April 1984

I

STUFF
&
NONSENSE

The Comedy of Lawyers

Some of the finest early examples of lawyers' comic wit come from the Irishman, John Philpot Curran, whose eloquence and conviviality made him famous throughout the British Isles in the late eighteenth and early nineteenth century. A notable example of Curran's style occurred when he was addressing a court in County Cork, one summer day in 1778.

Suddenly, in the middle of his speech, the unmistakable sound of an ass braying drifted into the building through an open window. The judge, knowing of Curran's reputation and hoping to profit at his expense, remarked: 'One at a time, Mr Curran, if you please.'

The lawyer made no mention of the incident until later when the judge was giving his address to the jury – and once again the ass gave out a particularly piteous bray.

At which Curran interjected, 'Does your Lordship not hear a remarkable echo in the court?'

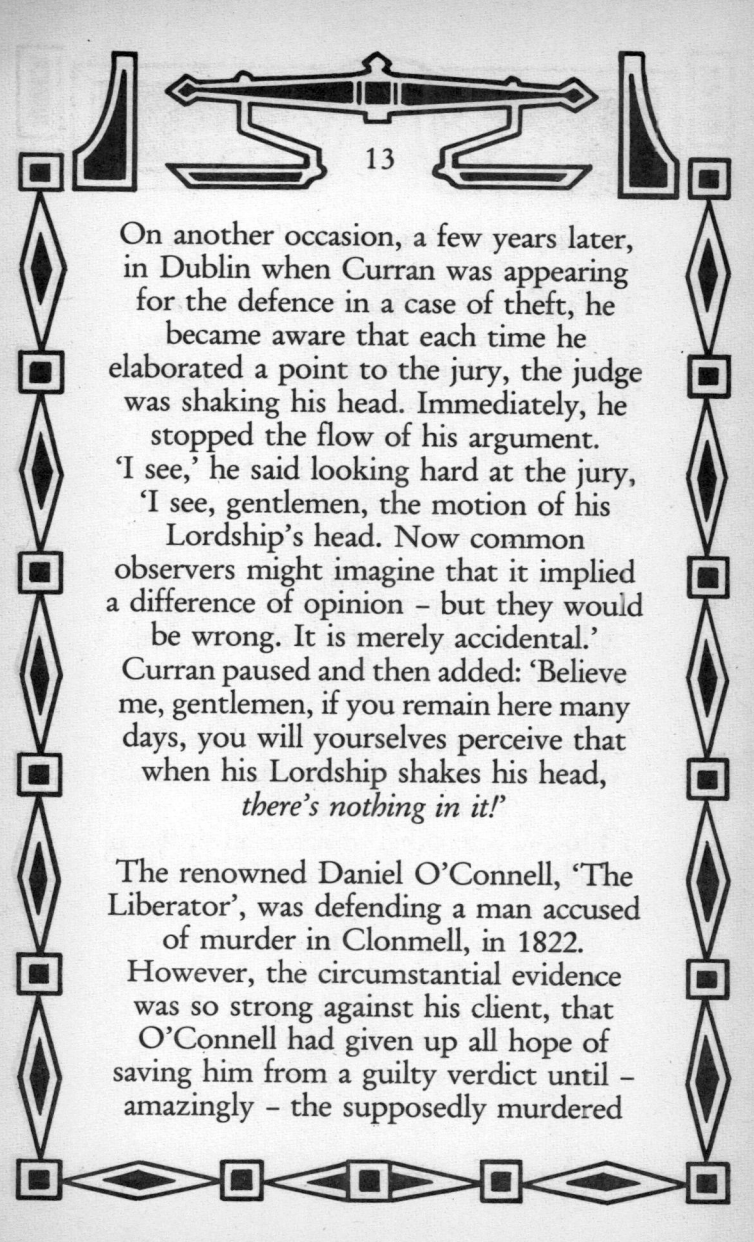

On another occasion, a few years later,
in Dublin when Curran was appearing
for the defence in a case of theft, he
became aware that each time he
elaborated a point to the jury, the judge
was shaking his head. Immediately, he
stopped the flow of his argument.
'I see,' he said looking hard at the jury,
'I see, gentlemen, the motion of his
Lordship's head. Now common
observers might imagine that it implied
a difference of opinion – but they would
be wrong. It is merely accidental.'
Curran paused and then added: 'Believe
me, gentlemen, if you remain here many
days, you will yourselves perceive that
when his Lordship shakes his head,
there's nothing in it!'

The renowned Daniel O'Connell, 'The
Liberator', was defending a man accused
of murder in Clonmell, in 1822.
However, the circumstantial evidence
was so strong against his client, that
O'Connell had given up all hope of
saving him from a guilty verdict until –
amazingly – the supposedly murdered

man appeared alive and well in the court room.

The jury were duly instructed to return a verdict of not guilty.

However, after retiring for some while, the foreman pronounced their decision: 'Guilty.'

O'Connell leapt to his feet. 'What do you mean?' he roared. 'If the man has not been murdered, how *can* the prisoner be guilty?'

'If it please you, sir,' the foreman replied, 'he's guilty. He's the one who stole my horse three years ago!'

A rakish young lawyer, David Thurlow, was accosted by a friend going into a London court in 1838.

'Thurlow,' the other solicitor said, 'I am told the barmaid at Nando's is with child.'

'Well, what is that to *me*?'

'Why, I am told it is yours.'

'Well,' exclaimed Thurlow, before striding on, 'what is that to *you*?'

Two solicitors were pressing their

respective claims in a boundary dispute before Lord Chancellor Hatton in London, in 1849.

'We lie on this side, my Lord,' said one man.

'And we lie on this side,' added the other.

'If you lie on both sides,' responded the venerable old judge, 'whom will you have me believe?'

A Boston lawyer, Rufus Choate, was cross-examining a seaman about a case of assault and battery which had taken place at sea in 1852. In the stand was Richard Barton, chief mate of the clipper ship, *Challenge*.

After some verbal sparring between the two men, Choate asked the witness:

'Now tell me in what latitude and longitude you crossed the equator?'

'Oh, you're joking!' came the response.

'No, sir, I am in earnest and I require an answer.'

'That's more than I can give.'

'Indeed?' said the lawyer. 'You are the chief mate of a clipper ship, and unable to answer so simple a question?'

'Yes,' replied Barton with an unmistakable gleam of triumph in his eyes, 'that's the simplest question I ever had asked me. I thought every fool of a lawyer knew there is no latitude at the equator!'

After the death of a very poor solicitor in Dublin during the middle of the last century, a 'shilling subscription' was set up to pay the expenses of his funeral – and to which most of the members of the legal profession in the city made donations.

An approach was also made to the irrascible Judge Norbury.

'Only a shilling?' said the judge. 'Only a shilling to bury a solicitor! Here is a guinea – go and bury twenty-one of them!'

Two Californian lawyers quarrelled in a bar, in the middle of the last century, and agreed that the only way to settle their differences was to fight a duel. This was thereafter promptly arranged.

However, both men were poor shots, one man missing the other completely, and the return shot only nicking the bottom of his rival's coat.

On observing his modest success, and realising the absurdity of what had occurred, the second man said: 'My friend, if you had been a client I would most certainly have hit you in the pocket!'

Randle Jackson, a London solicitor renowned for his eloquence rather than his use of legal precedents when conducting cases, met his match in 1858 when he was representing the East India Company before Chief Justice Lord Ellenborough.

'In the book of nature, my Lord,' Jackson declared after a particularly lengthy and forceful diatribe, 'it is written ——'

Before he could go any further, Lord Ellenborough held up his hand and asked gravely, 'Will you have the goodness to mention the page, sir, if you please?'

During a long and complex case in Colorado in 1869, two American lawyers, David Parsons and Frank Sullivan, engaged in a great deal of point scoring off each other, as well as the occasional practical joke.

At one point, while Parsons was delivering a lengthy and emotional plea, Sullivan surreptitiously picked up his rival's large black hat from beneath the bench where they were sitting, and wrote on it with a piece of chalk: 'This is the hat of a Damned Rascal.'

It was not until other people sitting around began to chuckle that David Parsons saw what had happened. But his quick wit did not desert him.

'May it please your Honour,' he addressed the judge, 'I crave the protection of the court. My learned friend has been stealing my hat – and writing his own name upon it!'

A Liverpool solicitor called upon another colleague in 1872 to seek his opinion about a certain point of law. Immediately the second man had been

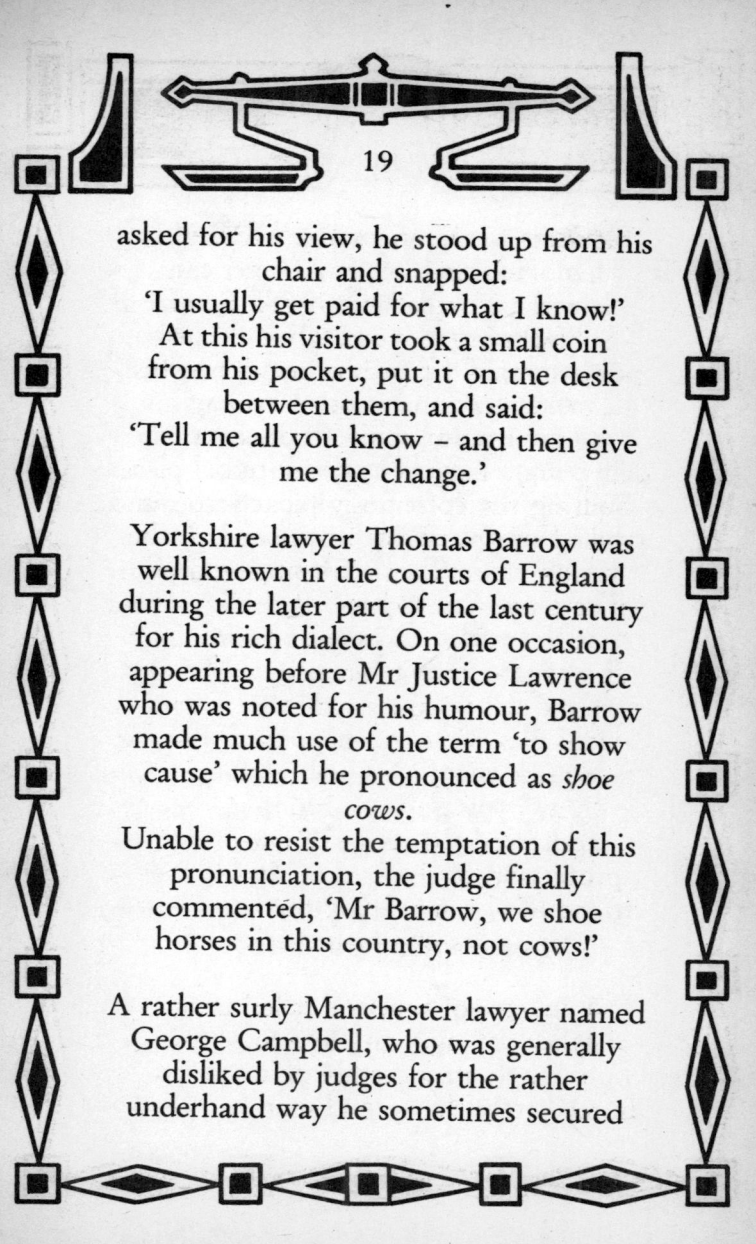

asked for his view, he stood up from his chair and snapped:
'I usually get paid for what I know!'
At this his visitor took a small coin from his pocket, put it on the desk between them, and said:
'Tell me all you know – and then give me the change.'

Yorkshire lawyer Thomas Barrow was well known in the courts of England during the later part of the last century for his rich dialect. On one occasion, appearing before Mr Justice Lawrence who was noted for his humour, Barrow made much use of the term 'to show cause' which he pronounced as *shoe cows*.
Unable to resist the temptation of this pronunciation, the judge finally commented, 'Mr Barrow, we shoe horses in this country, not cows!'

A rather surly Manchester lawyer named George Campbell, who was generally disliked by judges for the rather underhand way he sometimes secured

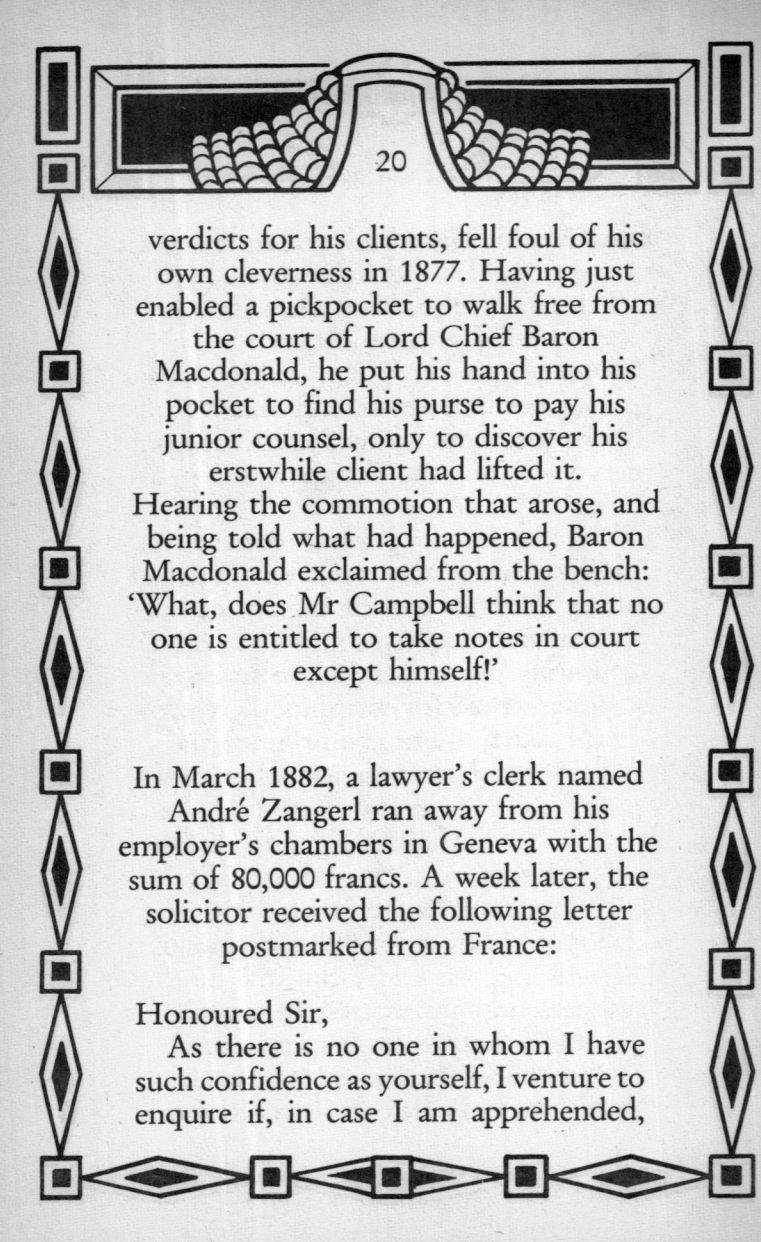

verdicts for his clients, fell foul of his own cleverness in 1877. Having just enabled a pickpocket to walk free from the court of Lord Chief Baron Macdonald, he put his hand into his pocket to find his purse to pay his junior counsel, only to discover his erstwhile client had lifted it.

Hearing the commotion that arose, and being told what had happened, Baron Macdonald exclaimed from the bench: 'What, does Mr Campbell think that no one is entitled to take notes in court except himself!'

In March 1882, a lawyer's clerk named André Zangerl ran away from his employer's chambers in Geneva with the sum of 80,000 francs. A week later, the solicitor received the following letter postmarked from France:

Honoured Sir,
As there is no one in whom I have such confidence as yourself, I venture to enquire if, in case I am apprehended,

you would consent to undertake my defence?

Yours very respectfully,
A. Zangerl

Lawyer Frank Bennett, who was noted for the intimidatory tactics he used on nervous witnesses, was appearing in a case of assault in London in 1883.
Cross-examining one of the eye-witnesses to the fight, he asked the man how close he was to the trouble.
'Just four feet and five and a half inches,' came the precise reply.
'How can you be so exact,' Bennett glared at the man in the box.
'Because I expected some fool or other would ask me, so I measured it!' was the reply.

Thomas Bravington, a Manchester solicitor renowned for the fervour of his pleading, was addressing the jury in a case brought in 1885, when his eloquence proved his undoing.
'Gentlemen of the jury,' Bravington exclaimed as he neared the end of his

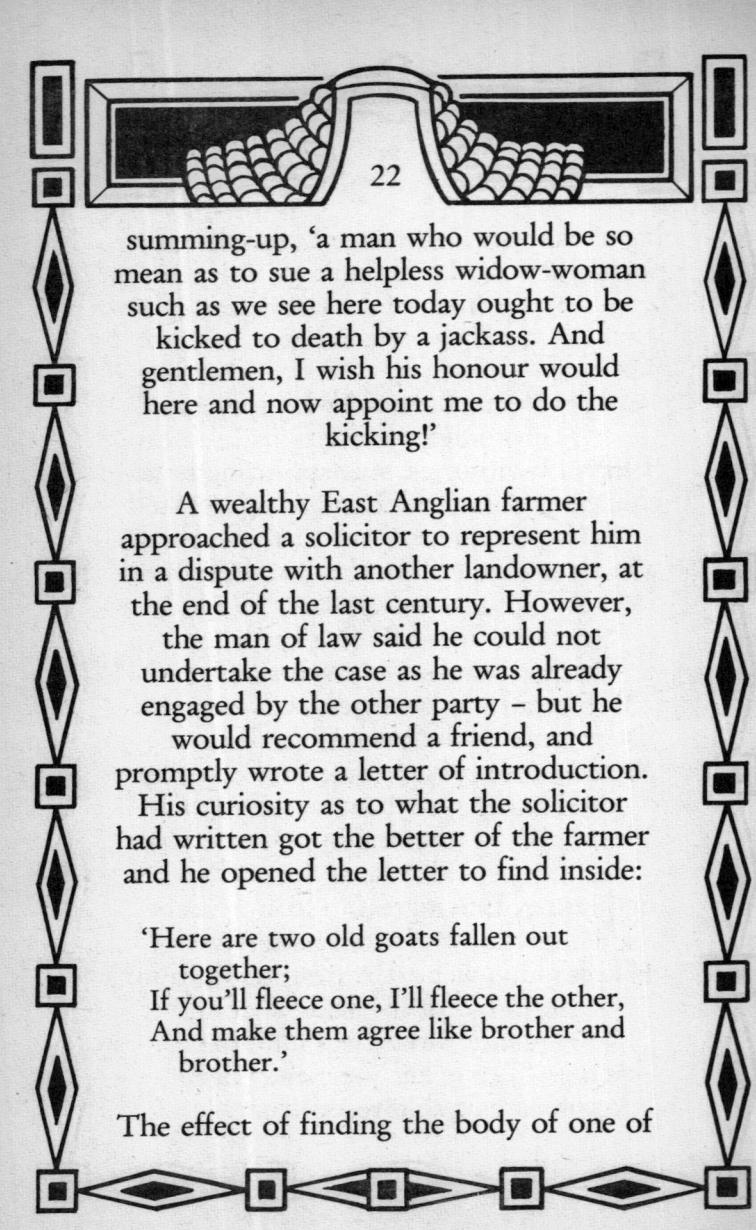

summing-up, 'a man who would be so mean as to sue a helpless widow-woman such as we see here today ought to be kicked to death by a jackass. And gentlemen, I wish his honour would here and now appoint me to do the kicking!'

A wealthy East Anglian farmer approached a solicitor to represent him in a dispute with another landowner, at the end of the last century. However, the man of law said he could not undertake the case as he was already engaged by the other party – but he would recommend a friend, and promptly wrote a letter of introduction. His curiosity as to what the solicitor had written got the better of the farmer and he opened the letter to find inside:

'Here are two old goats fallen out
   together;
If you'll fleece one, I'll fleece the other,
And make them agree like brother and
   brother.'

The effect of finding the body of one of

his clerks who had hanged himself in his chambers, made the eminent solicitor, John Williams, of Lincolns Inn in London, very cautious when it came to appointing another in 1890. Indeed, he is reported to have told the successful applicant:

'I have one more stipulation to make to you. Should you decide to hang yourself – which you can do or not as you think fit – pray do not hang yourself in my chambers!'

The jovial Scottish lawyer, Harold McKenna, was pleading the case of a lady client named Tickle in a Dundee court case in the closing years of the last century.

Never one to miss the opportunity for a little fun, McKenna opened his remarks with a wave of his arm in the direction of the witness box.

'Tickle my client, the defendant, my Lord,' he said.

The judge, however, was a match for his wit: 'Tickle her yourself, Harry – you are as able to do it as I!'

In remitting his bill of costs for conducting a lady's divorce case, a German solicitor at the end of the last century included this item: 'Further, 30 marks, for being awoken in the night and having thought over your case.'

In the 1890s during his early days as lawyer, the famous American attorney, Joseph Hodges Choate, received a client in his chambers who was in litigation over a boundary dispute.

The man told Choate: 'It's like this. There is a fence that runs between Brown's place and mine. He claims that I encroach on his land, and I insist that he is trespassing on mine. Now what would you recommend?'

'Well,' said Choate, 'if I were in your place, I'd go over and give Brown a drink and settle the dispute in ten minutes. But, as things are, I advise you to sue him. Let no arrogant, domineering, insolent pirate like Brown trample on your sacred rights! Assert your manhood and your courage. And I need the money!'

When he was a youngster, the famous American lawyer, Chauncey Mitchell Depew, bought a spotted dog from a local pet-dealer. The following day when he took the dog for a walk it was raining, and as the animal ran alongside him the spots gradually washed away.

Depew hurried back to the dealer. 'Look at this animal,' he said. 'The spots have washed off!'

Not in the least perturbed, the man said: 'Great guns, boy! There was an umbrella went with that dog. Didn't you get the umbrella?'

The brilliant wit of F. E. Smith made him an enduring legend in legal circles – both for his humour in court and out of it.

Attending a glittering social gathering in London one day early this century, his attention was drawn to a young woman who was wearing a very scanty dress which revealed almost all of her very full bosom.

'Oh,' he said in reply to a request as to whether he knew her, 'that is a

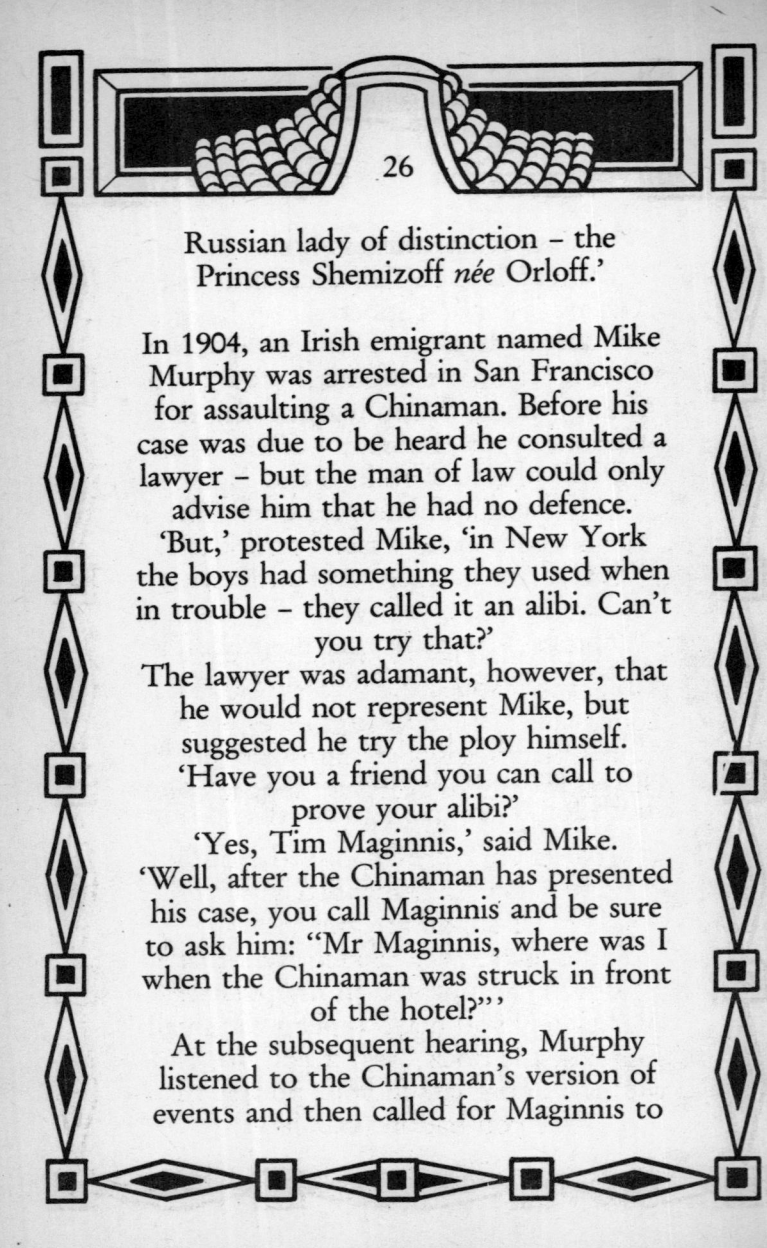

Russian lady of distinction – the
Princess Shemizoff *née* Orloff.'

In 1904, an Irish emigrant named Mike
Murphy was arrested in San Francisco
for assaulting a Chinaman. Before his
case was due to be heard he consulted a
lawyer – but the man of law could only
advise him that he had no defence.
'But,' protested Mike, 'in New York
the boys had something they used when
in trouble – they called it an alibi. Can't
you try that?'
The lawyer was adamant, however, that
he would not represent Mike, but
suggested he try the ploy himself.
'Have you a friend you can call to
prove your alibi?'
'Yes, Tim Maginnis,' said Mike.
'Well, after the Chinaman has presented
his case, you call Maginnis and be sure
to ask him: "Mr Maginnis, where was I
when the Chinaman was struck in front
of the hotel?"'
At the subsequent hearing, Murphy
listened to the Chinaman's version of
events and then called for Maginnis to

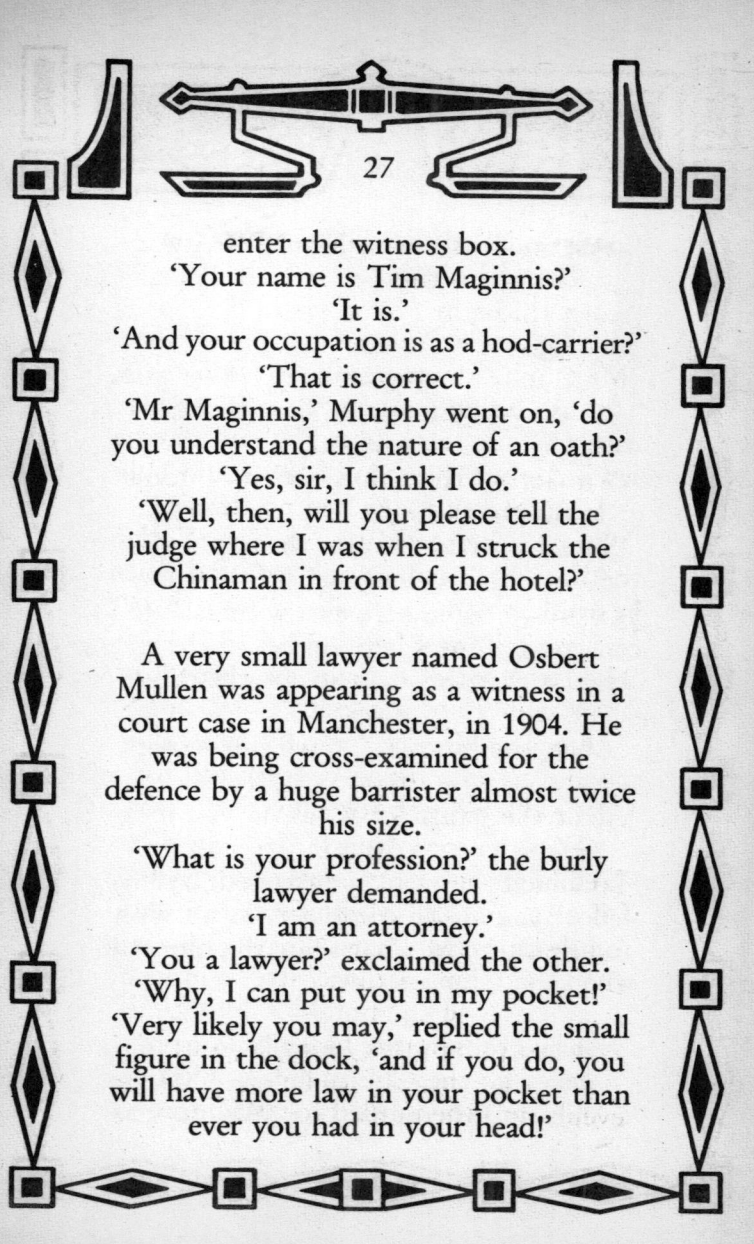

enter the witness box.
'Your name is Tim Maginnis?'
'It is.'
'And your occupation is as a hod-carrier?'
'That is correct.'
'Mr Maginnis,' Murphy went on, 'do
you understand the nature of an oath?'
'Yes, sir, I think I do.'
'Well, then, will you please tell the
judge where I was when I struck the
Chinaman in front of the hotel?'

A very small lawyer named Osbert
Mullen was appearing as a witness in a
court case in Manchester, in 1904. He
was being cross-examined for the
defence by a huge barrister almost twice
his size.
'What is your profession?' the burly
lawyer demanded.
'I am an attorney.'
'You a lawyer?' exclaimed the other.
'Why, I can put you in my pocket!'
'Very likely you may,' replied the small
figure in the dock, 'and if you do, you
will have more law in your pocket than
ever you had in your head!'

A London seaman, John Cook, was called as a witness in a court case at Rotherhithe in 1905 about a dispute at sea.

'Mr Cook,' the prosecuting lawyer said, 'do you know the plaintiff and defendant?'

'I'm sorry,' the sailor replied, 'I don't know the meaning of them words.'

'What! You don't know the meaning of plaintiff and defendant! A fine fellow you are to come here as a witness! Well, can you tell me where on board the ship it was that this man struck the other one?'

'Abaft the binnacle,' came the prompt reply.

'Abaft the binnacle? What do you mean by that?'

To which the seaman answered: 'A fine fellow *you* are to come here as a lawyer and don't know what abaft the binnacle means!'

A rather bumptious young lawyer came into the witness box before Judge Collins in Birmingham, in 1906, to give testimony as an expert.

'I wish to ask the court,' he said, 'if I am compelled to come into this case, in which I have no personal interest, and give a legal opinion for nothing?'

'Yes, certainly,' replied the astute Judge Collins, 'give it for what it is worth!'

William 'Wittering Billy' Martin, a London solicitor of very humble origins, who made full use of his Cockney language and wit when pleading cases, appeared for a Marylebone shopkeeper in a complex property dispute, in 1908. Having addressed the judge and jury for some hours on the case, Martin sat down to allow his junior counsel to sum up. 'Ladies and gentlemen of the jury,' the young man said rather hesitantly, 'considering the length of my learned leader's remarks, I will not weary the court with an address of my own – except only to add the "h's"!'

A Norfolk shopkeeper went to see a solicitor in Norwich, in 1910, for advice.

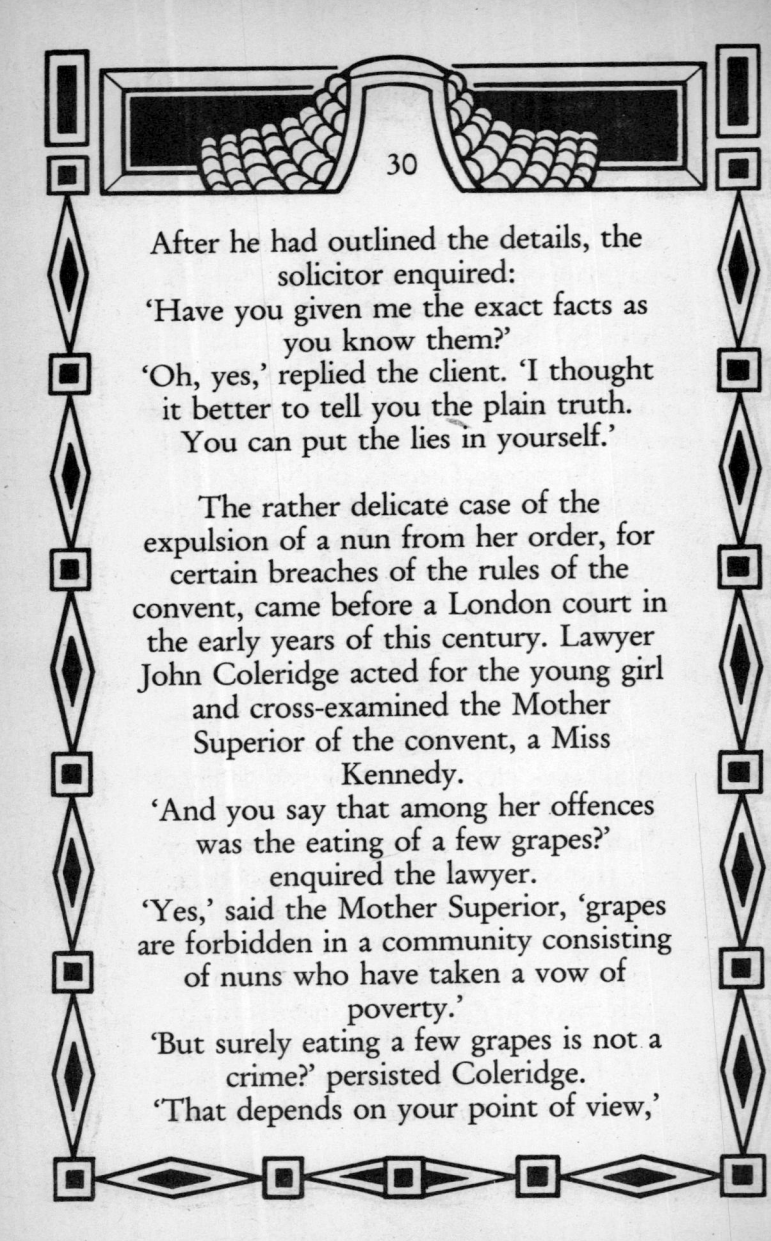

After he had outlined the details, the solicitor enquired:
'Have you given me the exact facts as you know them?'
'Oh, yes,' replied the client. 'I thought it better to tell you the plain truth. You can put the lies in yourself.'

The rather delicate case of the expulsion of a nun from her order, for certain breaches of the rules of the convent, came before a London court in the early years of this century. Lawyer John Coleridge acted for the young girl and cross-examined the Mother Superior of the convent, a Miss Kennedy.
'And you say that among her offences was the eating of a few grapes?' enquired the lawyer.
'Yes,' said the Mother Superior, 'grapes are forbidden in a community consisting of nuns who have taken a vow of poverty.'
'But surely eating a few grapes is not a crime?' persisted Coleridge.
'That depends on your point of view,'

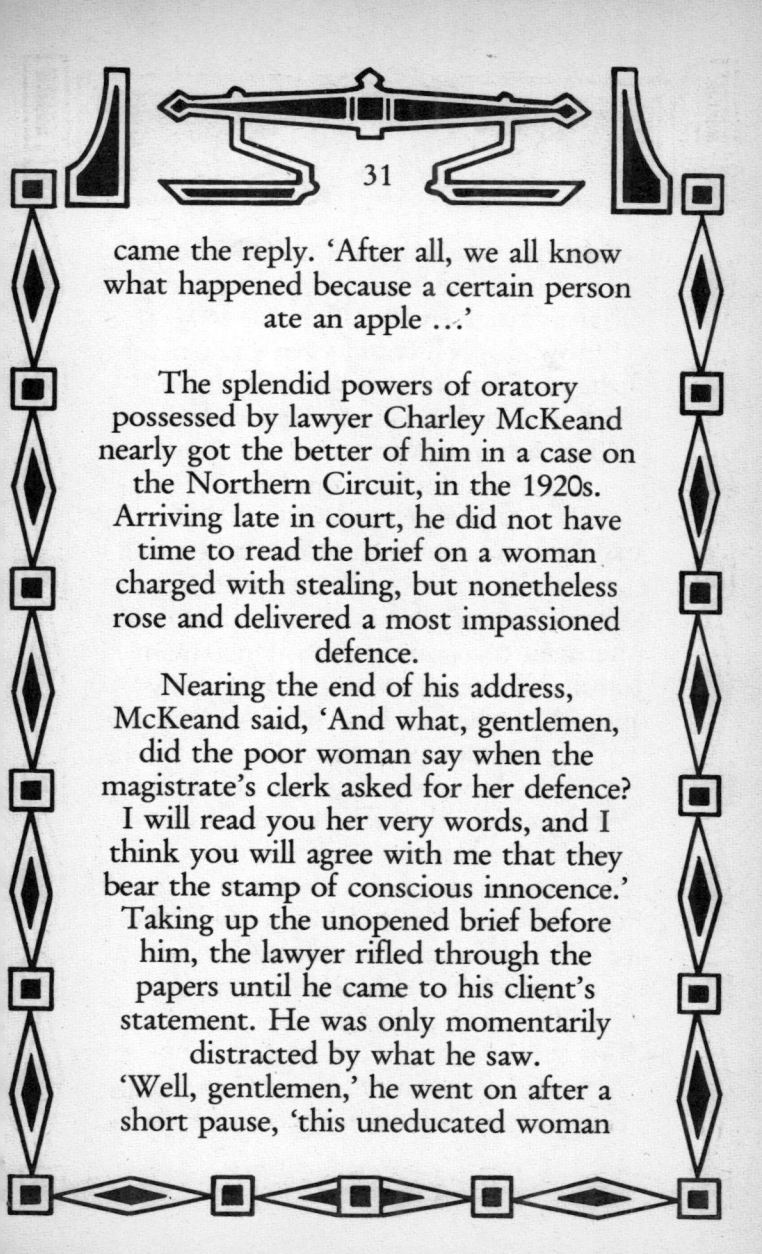

came the reply. 'After all, we all know what happened because a certain person ate an apple ...'

The splendid powers of oratory possessed by lawyer Charley McKeand nearly got the better of him in a case on the Northern Circuit, in the 1920s. Arriving late in court, he did not have time to read the brief on a woman charged with stealing, but nonetheless rose and delivered a most impassioned defence.

Nearing the end of his address, McKeand said, 'And what, gentlemen, did the poor woman say when the magistrate's clerk asked for her defence? I will read you her very words, and I think you will agree with me that they bear the stamp of conscious innocence.' Taking up the unopened brief before him, the lawyer rifled through the papers until he came to his client's statement. He was only momentarily distracted by what he saw.

'Well, gentlemen,' he went on after a short pause, 'this uneducated woman

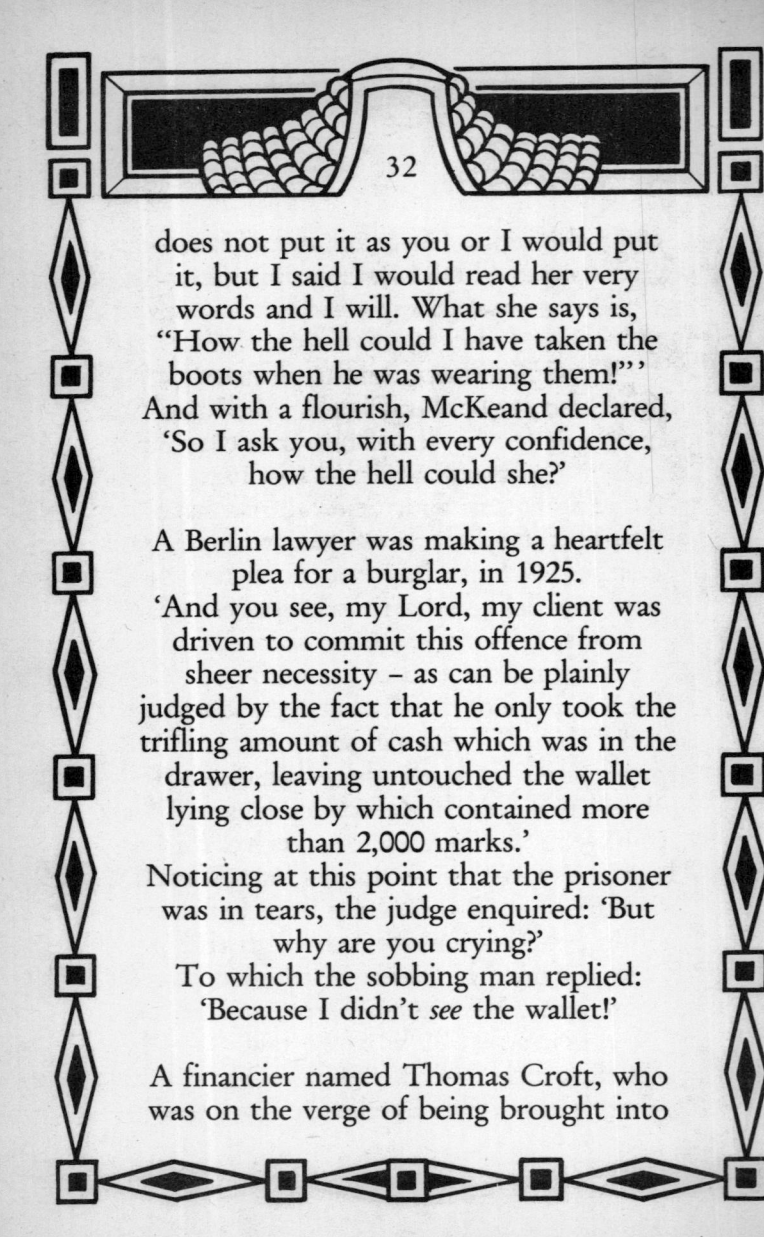

does not put it as you or I would put it, but I said I would read her very words and I will. What she says is, "How the hell could I have taken the boots when he was wearing them!"'
And with a flourish, McKeand declared, 'So I ask you, with every confidence, how the hell could she?'

A Berlin lawyer was making a heartfelt plea for a burglar, in 1925.
'And you see, my Lord, my client was driven to commit this offence from sheer necessity – as can be plainly judged by the fact that he only took the trifling amount of cash which was in the drawer, leaving untouched the wallet lying close by which contained more than 2,000 marks.'
Noticing at this point that the prisoner was in tears, the judge enquired: 'But why are you crying?'
To which the sobbing man replied: 'Because I didn't *see* the wallet!'

A financier named Thomas Croft, who was on the verge of being brought into

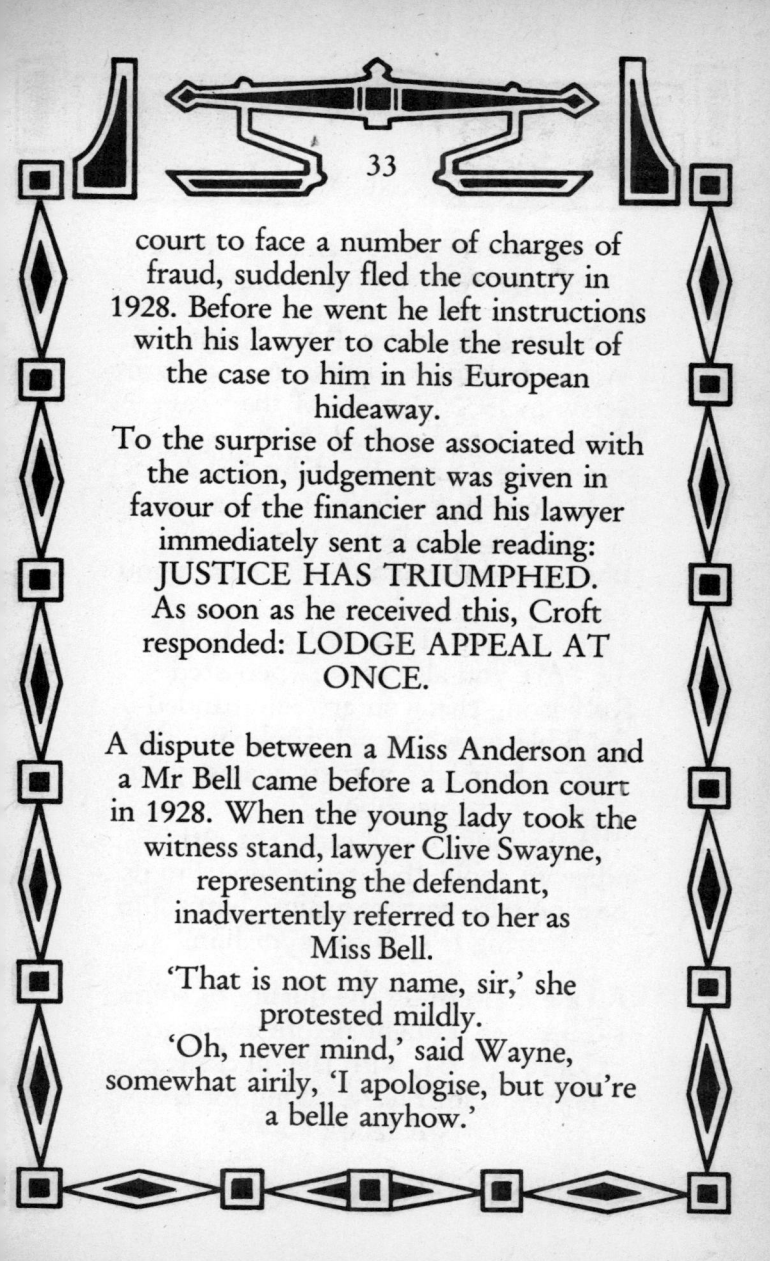

court to face a number of charges of fraud, suddenly fled the country in 1928. Before he went he left instructions with his lawyer to cable the result of the case to him in his European hideaway.

To the surprise of those associated with the action, judgement was given in favour of the financier and his lawyer immediately sent a cable reading: JUSTICE HAS TRIUMPHED.

As soon as he received this, Croft responded: LODGE APPEAL AT ONCE.

A dispute between a Miss Anderson and a Mr Bell came before a London court in 1928. When the young lady took the witness stand, lawyer Clive Swayne, representing the defendant, inadvertently referred to her as Miss Bell.

'That is not my name, sir,' she protested mildly.

'Oh, never mind,' said Wayne, somewhat airily, 'I apologise, but you're a belle anyhow.'

'Then I suppose,' came the quick response, 'you are my loving swain!'

The English lawyer, Peter Robinson, was examining a witness in a court in Kerry, in 1930. Because of the nature of the man's replies, Robinson began to have grave doubts about his testimony. After one particularly evasive answer, the lawyer asked: 'Do you fully understand the nature of the oath you have taken?'

'I do, sir.'

'Are you also aware,' persisted Robinson, 'that you are commanded in the Bible on which you took your oath not to bear false witness against your neighbour?'

'I am indeed, sir,' came the rather indignant reply, 'but to be sure, I'm not bearing false witness against him – I'm bearing false witness *for* him!'

A case concerning the quality of some timber was brought before a Glasgow Court in 1931, with the quicksilver lawyer, Tim Healy, acting for the defence.

During the course of the hearing, a young man was put in the witness box as an expert on the plaintiff's side. After he had given his evidence, lawyer Healy rose to his feet.

'What age are you?' he enquired.

'Twenty-one,' came the somewhat puzzled reply.

'And how long have you been in the timber trade?'

'Two years.'

At this Healy sat down, remarking as he did so, 'A regular babe in the wood, my Lord.'

A Colchester, Essex, solicitor was giving advice to a female client shortly after the death of her husband.

'My dear madam, I find that your estate is heavily encumbered,' he said. 'You will have enough to live upon, but you must husband your resources.'

'Well, my daughter Mary is my only resource now,' replied the good woman.

'Exactly,' added the attorney. 'Husband her as soon as possible!'

Two members of the London legal
profession, a lawyer and a judge, were
discussing the theory that the souls of
men could be transmogrified into
animals.

'Now,' said the judge, 'supposing you
and I could be turned into a horse or an
ass, which would you prefer to be?'

'Why, the ass to be sure,' said the
lawyer instantly.

The judge looked puzzled and asked his
friend why.

'Because I have heard of an ass being a
judge,' he said, 'but of a horse – never!'

A Bradford, Yorkshire, lawyer was
questioning a client in his chambers, in
1952, over the non-payment of a bill.

'And did you present the bill to Mr
Williams?' he said.

'Yes, I did.'

'And what did he say?'

'He told me to go to the devil.'

'And what did you do then?' the lawyer
added.

'Why, I came to see you!'

A veteran lawyer was talking to his young clerk in a London court some years ago during an adjournment. Glancing at the jurors sitting across the room, he indicated one particular man.

'It is easy to see that he has never served on a jury before,' said the lawyer.

'How?' enquired the puzzled junior.

'Because he pays such close attention to the evidence!'

II

SILK CUTS

The Humour of Barristers

One of eighteenth-century France's most famous advocates, Pierre Langlois, was asked one day by the President of the Parliament of Paris why he took it upon himself to plead on behalf of so many bad causes.

'Because, my Lord President,' he replied with a smile, 'I have lost a great many good ones!'

On the opening day of an important trial for murder in Dublin, in 1819, the well-known Irish barrister, Peter Burrowes, was stricken with a very heavy cold. As he was prosecuting the case, he supplied himself with a large number of throat lozenges to ease his congestion.

As he made his opening remarks, Burrowes popped the occasional lozenge into his mouth. And to emphasise his words he also held up the small bullet by which the murder victim had died.

Lozenge followed lozenge into the lawyer's mouth until, in the middle of a most emphatic declaration, he stopped. Then, clasping his throat, he gasped:

'My Lord. Gentlemen of the Jury. I've swallowed the bullet!'

During a dinner in 1839 at which the Dean of Ely, the Reverend Doctor Pease, was present, there was a lengthy discussion among the guests about the recent mortality rate of local lawyers. 'We have lost,' remarked one diner, 'not less than six eminent barristers in as many months.'
The Dean, who was quite deaf, seeing the conversation stop at this news, rose and instantly gave the company grace. 'For this and every other mercy,' he said, 'make us truly thankful.'

A very small barrister named George Morgan earned the nickname of 'Frog Morgan' because of his reliance on the Croke Law Reports, and the use of them to the virtual exclusion of all other authorities.
Nor was this name the only thing that earned him a place in the history of legal humour. For in 1843, appearing before Lord Mansfield, he suddenly

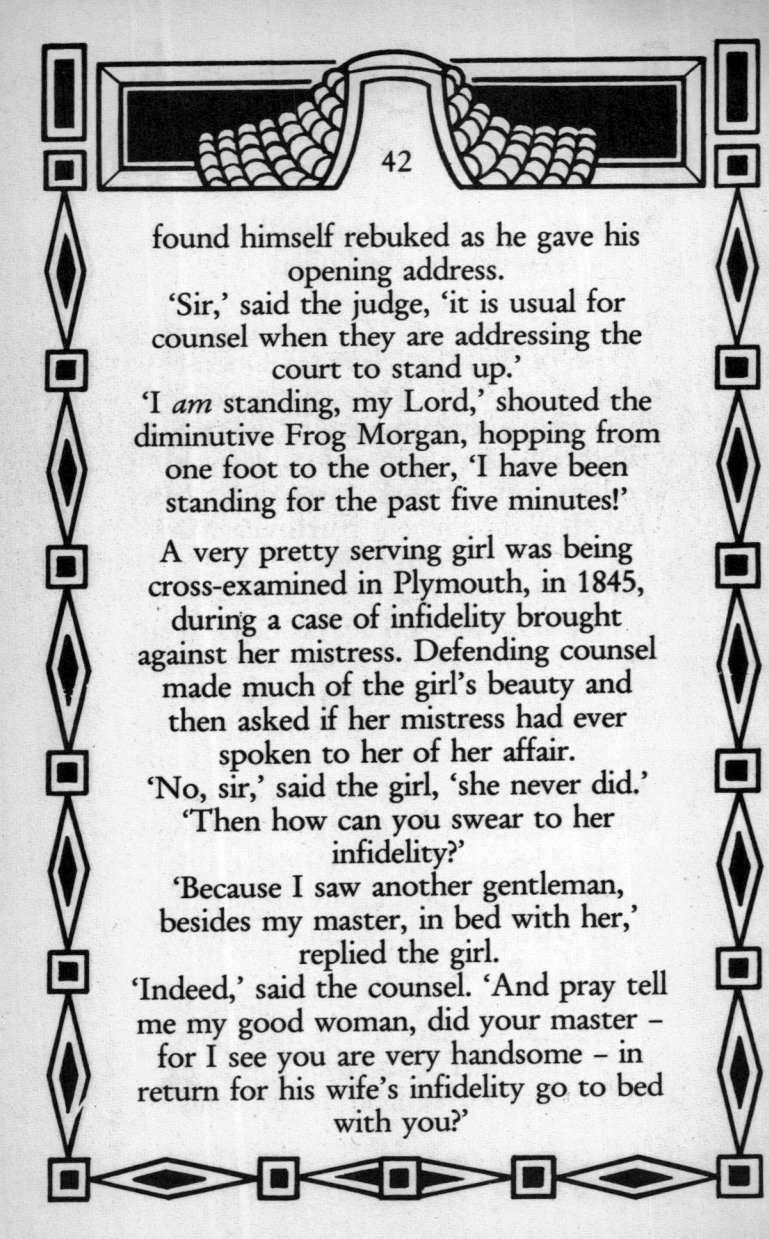

found himself rebuked as he gave his opening address.

'Sir,' said the judge, 'it is usual for counsel when they are addressing the court to stand up.'

'I *am* standing, my Lord,' shouted the diminutive Frog Morgan, hopping from one foot to the other, 'I have been standing for the past five minutes!'

A very pretty serving girl was being cross-examined in Plymouth, in 1845, during a case of infidelity brought against her mistress. Defending counsel made much of the girl's beauty and then asked if her mistress had ever spoken to her of her affair.

'No, sir,' said the girl, 'she never did.'

'Then how can you swear to her infidelity?'

'Because I saw another gentleman, besides my master, in bed with her,' replied the girl.

'Indeed,' said the counsel. 'And pray tell me my good woman, did your master – for I see you are very handsome – in return for his wife's infidelity go to bed with you?'

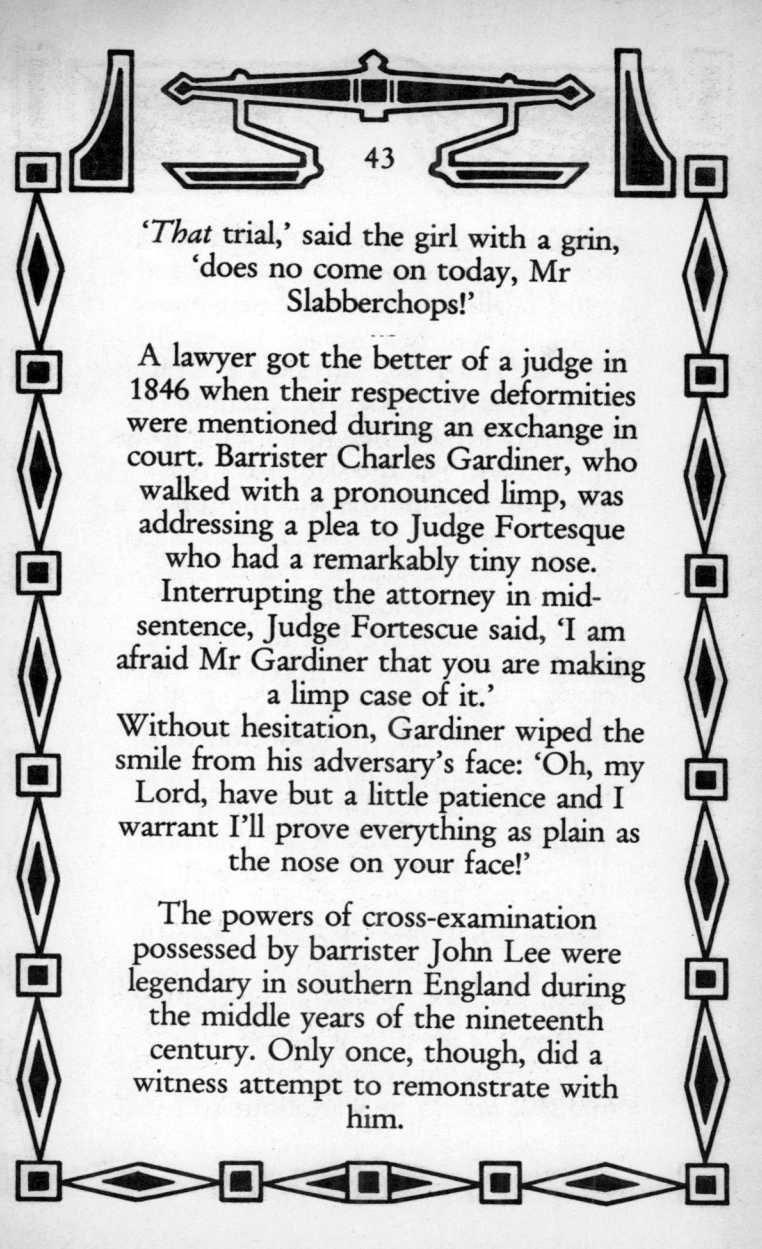

'*That* trial,' said the girl with a grin, 'does no come on today, Mr Slabberchops!'

A lawyer got the better of a judge in 1846 when their respective deformities were mentioned during an exchange in court. Barrister Charles Gardiner, who walked with a pronounced limp, was addressing a plea to Judge Fortesque who had a remarkably tiny nose.

Interrupting the attorney in mid-sentence, Judge Fortescue said, 'I am afraid Mr Gardiner that you are making a limp case of it.'

Without hesitation, Gardiner wiped the smile from his adversary's face: 'Oh, my Lord, have but a little patience and I warrant I'll prove everything as plain as the nose on your face!'

The powers of cross-examination possessed by barrister John Lee were legendary in southern England during the middle years of the nineteenth century. Only once, though, did a witness attempt to remonstrate with him.

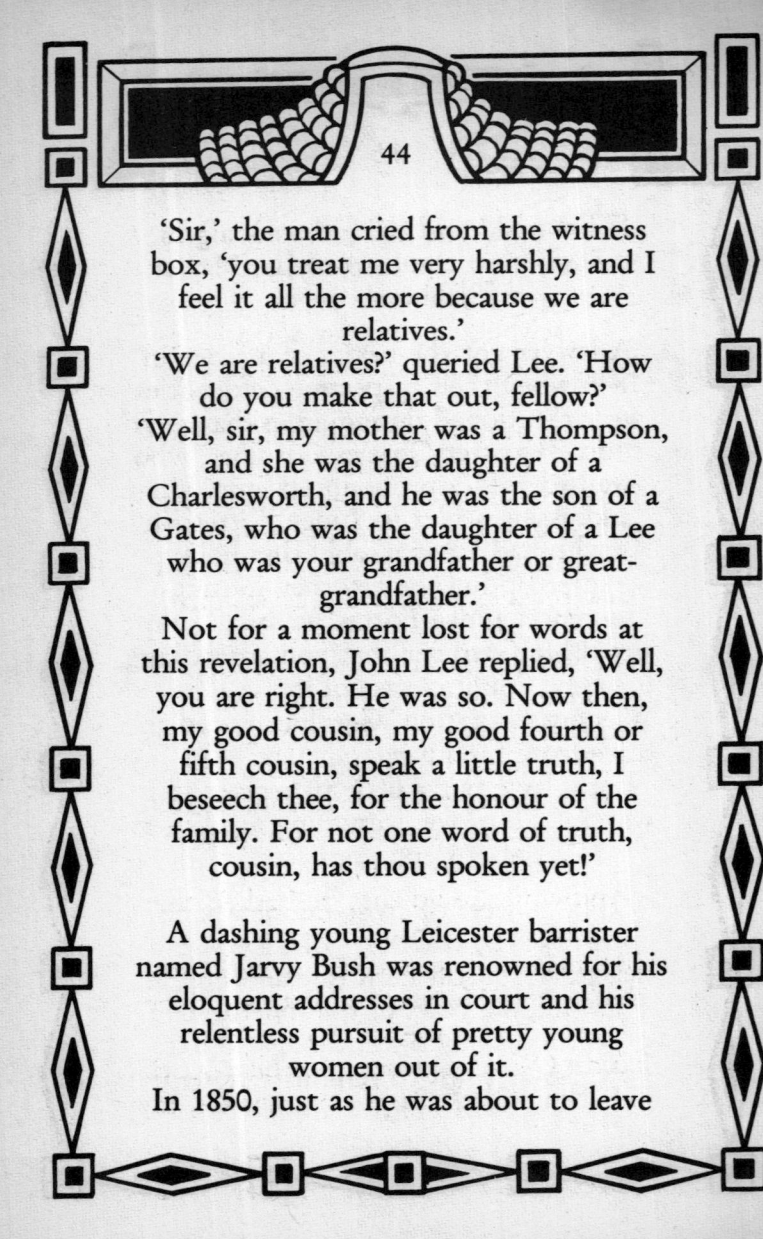

'Sir,' the man cried from the witness box, 'you treat me very harshly, and I feel it all the more because we are relatives.'

'We are relatives?' queried Lee. 'How do you make that out, fellow?'

'Well, sir, my mother was a Thompson, and she was the daughter of a Charlesworth, and he was the son of a Gates, who was the daughter of a Lee who was your grandfather or great-grandfather.'

Not for a moment lost for words at this revelation, John Lee replied, 'Well, you are right. He was so. Now then, my good cousin, my good fourth or fifth cousin, speak a little truth, I beseech thee, for the honour of the family. For not one word of truth, cousin, has thou spoken yet!'

A dashing young Leicester barrister named Jarvy Bush was renowned for his eloquent addresses in court and his relentless pursuit of pretty young women out of it.

In 1850, just as he was about to leave

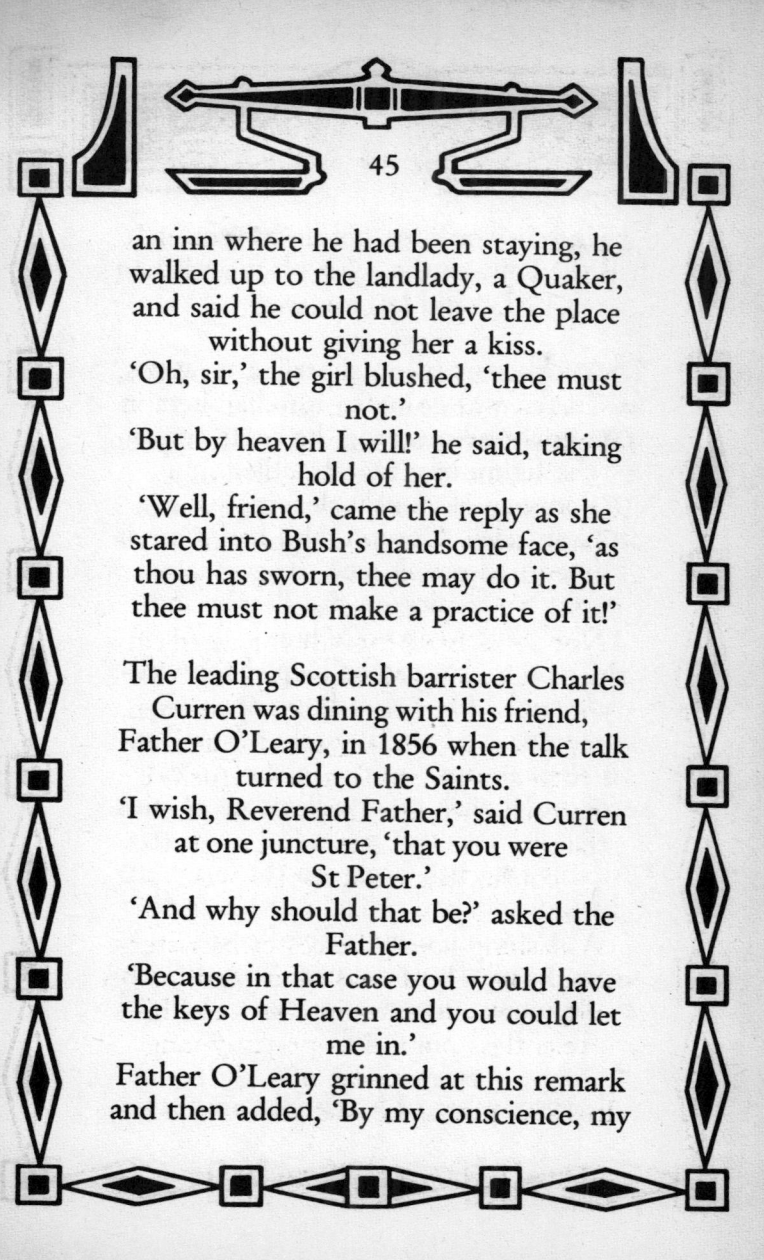

an inn where he had been staying, he
walked up to the landlady, a Quaker,
and said he could not leave the place
without giving her a kiss.

'Oh, sir,' the girl blushed, 'thee must
not.'

'But by heaven I will!' he said, taking
hold of her.

'Well, friend,' came the reply as she
stared into Bush's handsome face, 'as
thou has sworn, thee may do it. But
thee must not make a practice of it!'

The leading Scottish barrister Charles
Curren was dining with his friend,
Father O'Leary, in 1856 when the talk
turned to the Saints.

'I wish, Reverend Father,' said Curren
at one juncture, 'that you were
St Peter.'

'And why should that be?' asked the
Father.

'Because in that case you would have
the keys of Heaven and you could let
me in.'

Father O'Leary grinned at this remark
and then added, 'By my conscience, my

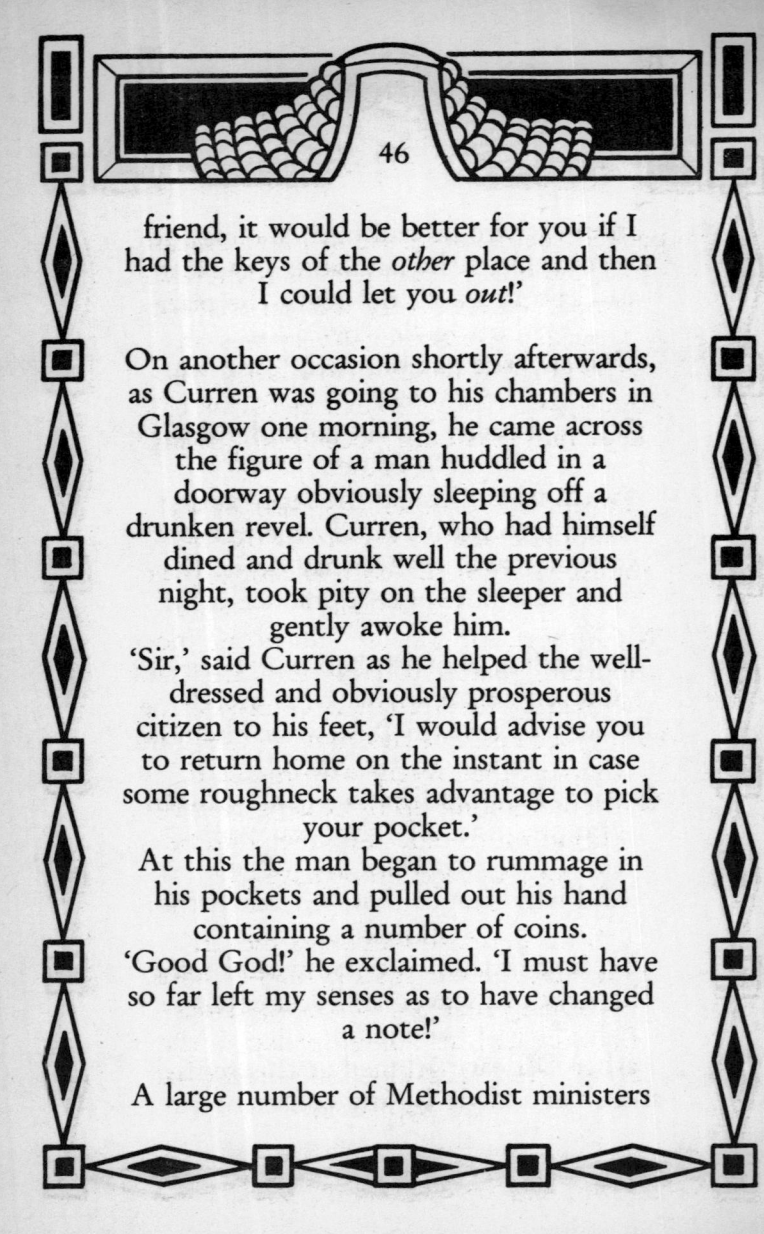

friend, it would be better for you if I had the keys of the *other* place and then I could let you *out*!'

On another occasion shortly afterwards, as Curren was going to his chambers in Glasgow one morning, he came across the figure of a man huddled in a doorway obviously sleeping off a drunken revel. Curren, who had himself dined and drunk well the previous night, took pity on the sleeper and gently awoke him.

'Sir,' said Curren as he helped the well-dressed and obviously prosperous citizen to his feet, 'I would advise you to return home on the instant in case some roughneck takes advantage to pick your pocket.'

At this the man began to rummage in his pockets and pulled out his hand containing a number of coins.

'Good God!' he exclaimed. 'I must have so far left my senses as to have changed a note!'

A large number of Methodist ministers

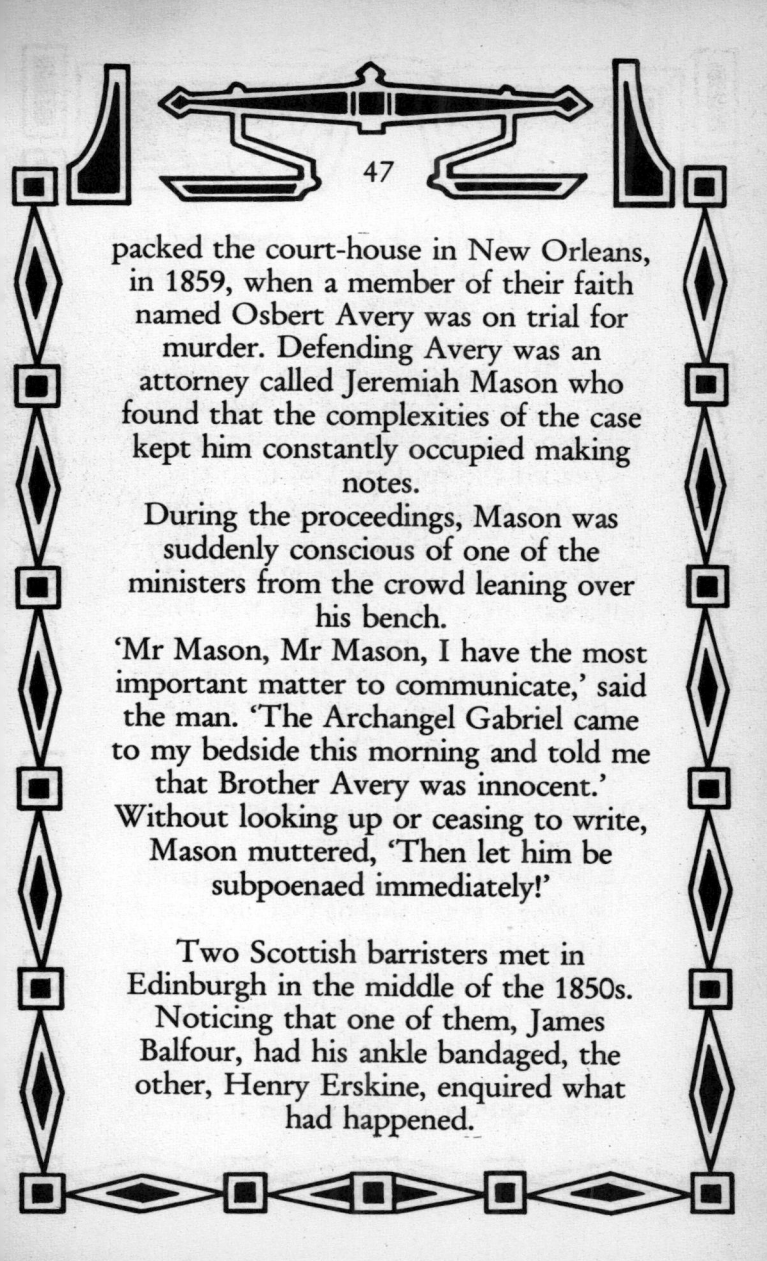

packed the court-house in New Orleans, in 1859, when a member of their faith named Osbert Avery was on trial for murder. Defending Avery was an attorney called Jeremiah Mason who found that the complexities of the case kept him constantly occupied making notes.

During the proceedings, Mason was suddenly conscious of one of the ministers from the crowd leaning over his bench.

'Mr Mason, Mr Mason, I have the most important matter to communicate,' said the man. 'The Archangel Gabriel came to my bedside this morning and told me that Brother Avery was innocent.'

Without looking up or ceasing to write, Mason muttered, 'Then let him be subpoenaed immediately!'

Two Scottish barristers met in Edinburgh in the middle of the 1850s. Noticing that one of them, James Balfour, had his ankle bandaged, the other, Henry Erskine, enquired what had happened.

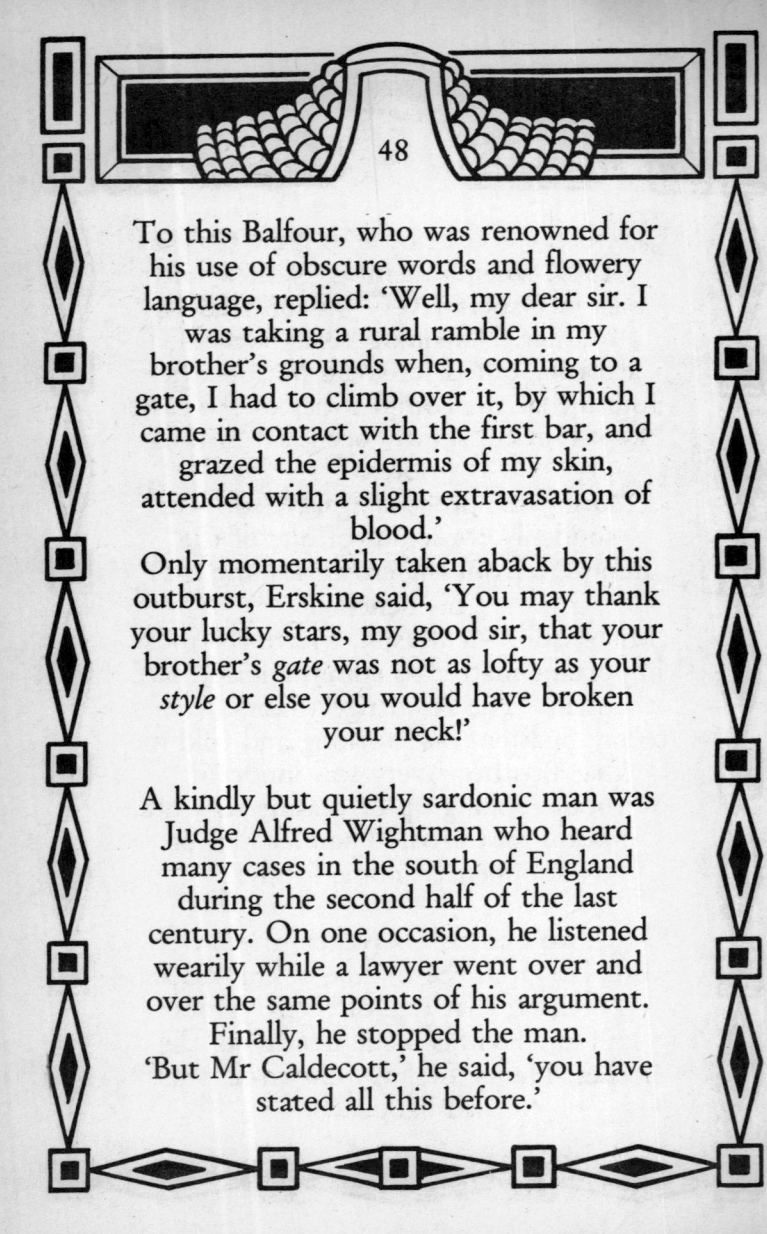

To this Balfour, who was renowned for his use of obscure words and flowery language, replied: 'Well, my dear sir. I was taking a rural ramble in my brother's grounds when, coming to a gate, I had to climb over it, by which I came in contact with the first bar, and grazed the epidermis of my skin, attended with a slight extravasation of blood.'

Only momentarily taken aback by this outburst, Erskine said, 'You may thank your lucky stars, my good sir, that your brother's *gate* was not as lofty as your *style* or else you would have broken your neck!'

A kindly but quietly sardonic man was Judge Alfred Wightman who heard many cases in the south of England during the second half of the last century. On one occasion, he listened wearily while a lawyer went over and over the same points of his argument. Finally, he stopped the man. 'But Mr Caldecott,' he said, 'you have stated all this before.'

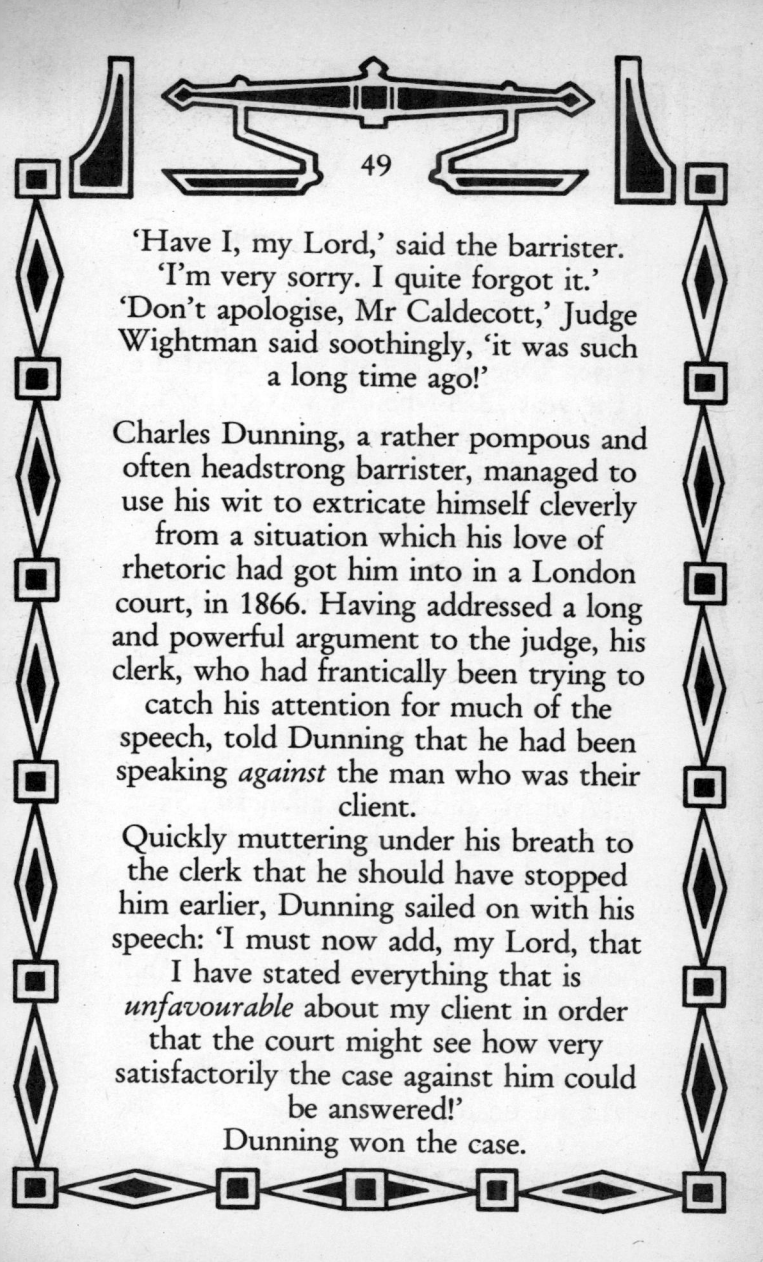

'Have I, my Lord,' said the barrister. 'I'm very sorry. I quite forgot it.' 'Don't apologise, Mr Caldecott,' Judge Wightman said soothingly, 'it was such a long time ago!'

Charles Dunning, a rather pompous and often headstrong barrister, managed to use his wit to extricate himself cleverly from a situation which his love of rhetoric had got him into in a London court, in 1866. Having addressed a long and powerful argument to the judge, his clerk, who had frantically been trying to catch his attention for much of the speech, told Dunning that he had been speaking *against* the man who was their client.

Quickly muttering under his breath to the clerk that he should have stopped him earlier, Dunning sailed on with his speech: 'I must now add, my Lord, that I have stated everything that is *unfavourable* about my client in order that the court might see how very satisfactorily the case against him could be answered!'

Dunning won the case.

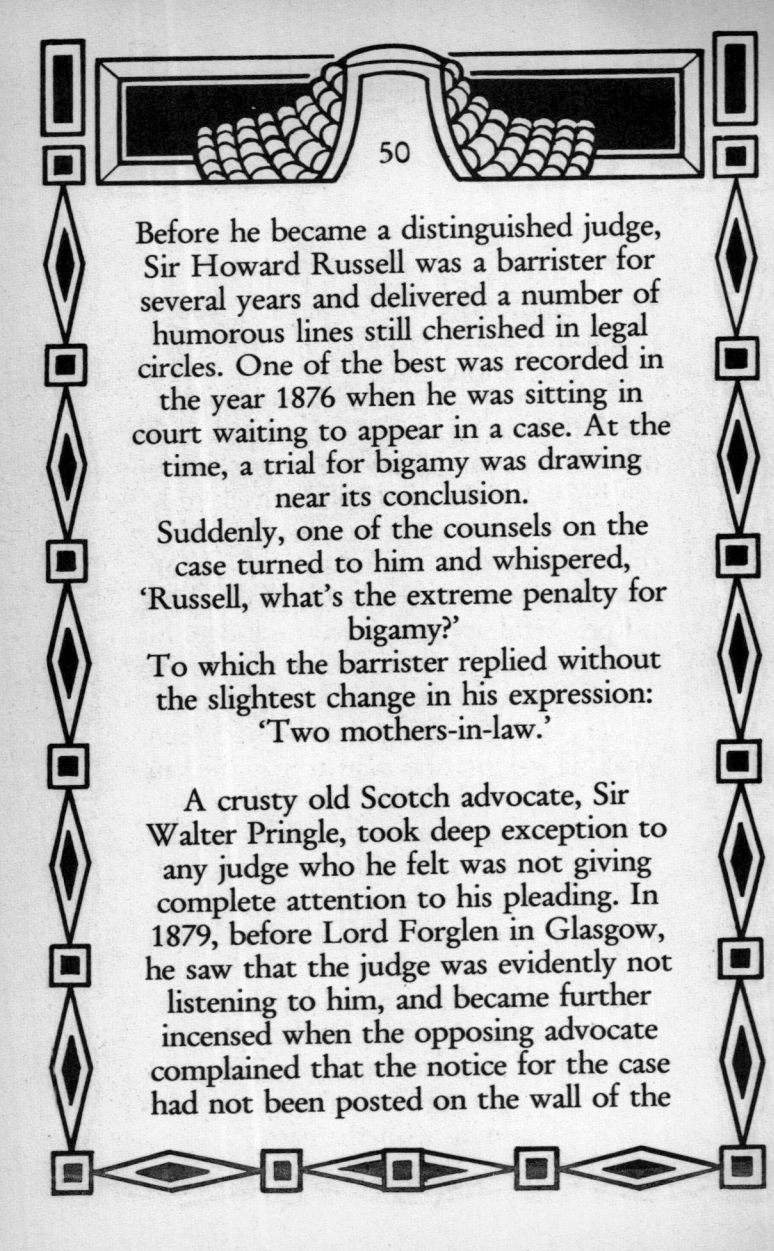

Before he became a distinguished judge, Sir Howard Russell was a barrister for several years and delivered a number of humorous lines still cherished in legal circles. One of the best was recorded in the year 1876 when he was sitting in court waiting to appear in a case. At the time, a trial for bigamy was drawing near its conclusion.

Suddenly, one of the counsels on the case turned to him and whispered, 'Russell, what's the extreme penalty for bigamy?'

To which the barrister replied without the slightest change in his expression: 'Two mothers-in-law.'

A crusty old Scotch advocate, Sir Walter Pringle, took deep exception to any judge who he felt was not giving complete attention to his pleading. In 1879, before Lord Forglen in Glasgow, he saw that the judge was evidently not listening to him, and became further incensed when the opposing advocate complained that the notice for the case had not been posted on the wall of the

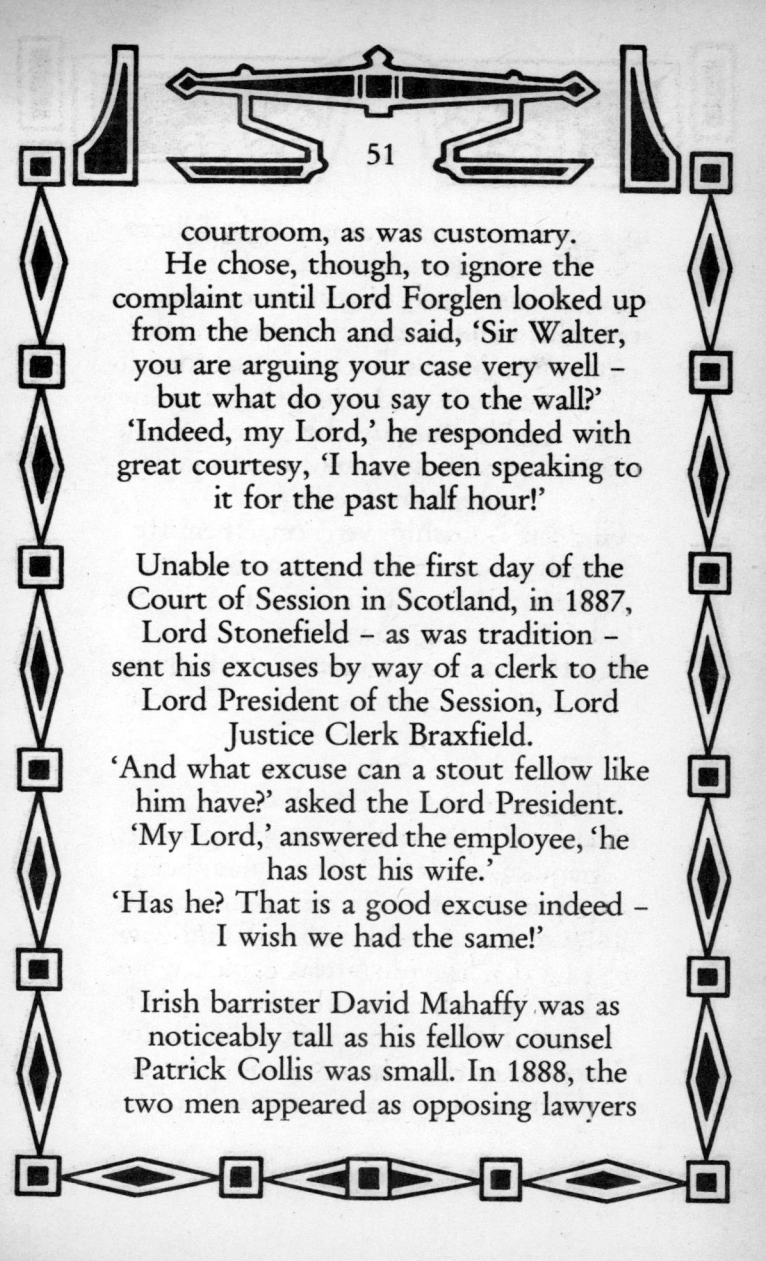

courtroom, as was customary.
He chose, though, to ignore the
complaint until Lord Forglen looked up
from the bench and said, 'Sir Walter,
you are arguing your case very well –
but what do you say to the wall?'
'Indeed, my Lord,' he responded with
great courtesy, 'I have been speaking to
it for the past half hour!'

Unable to attend the first day of the
Court of Session in Scotland, in 1887,
Lord Stonefield – as was tradition –
sent his excuses by way of a clerk to the
Lord President of the Session, Lord
Justice Clerk Braxfield.
'And what excuse can a stout fellow like
him have?' asked the Lord President.
'My Lord,' answered the employee, 'he
has lost his wife.'
'Has he? That is a good excuse indeed –
I wish we had the same!'

Irish barrister David Mahaffy was as
noticeably tall as his fellow counsel
Patrick Collis was small. In 1888, the
two men appeared as opposing lawyers

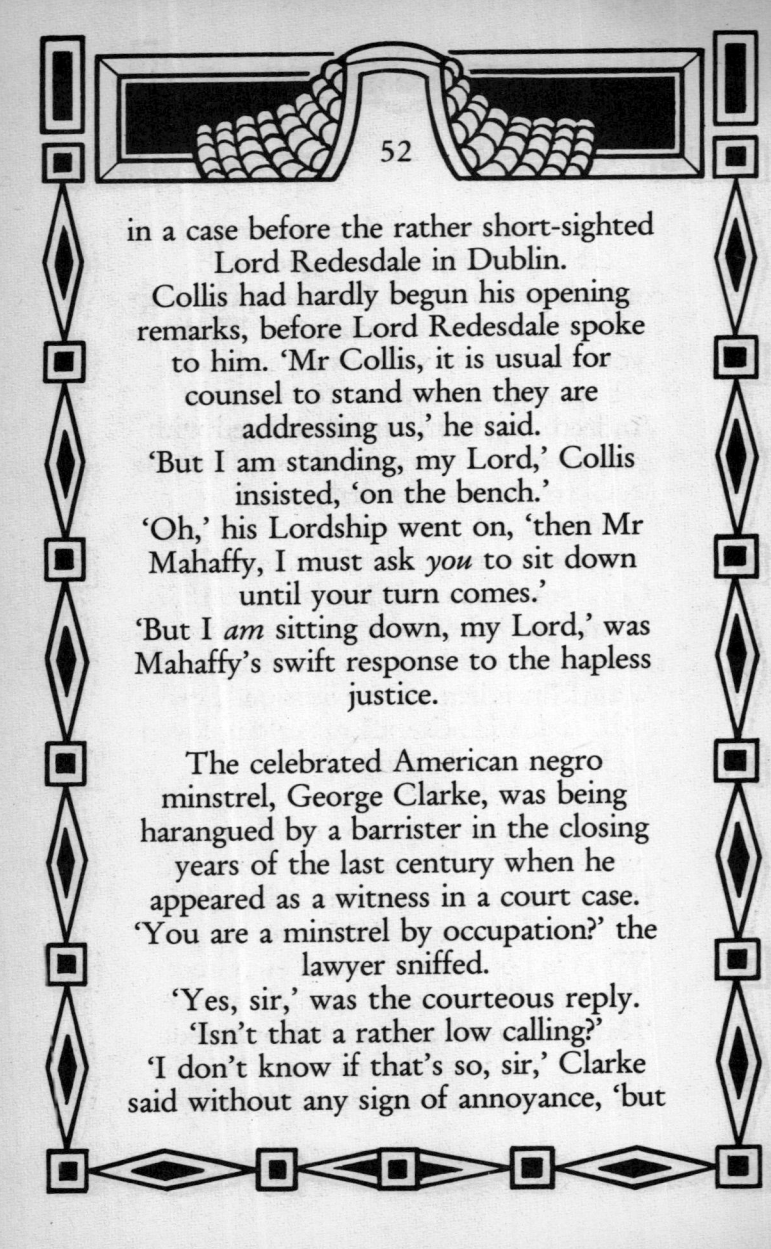

in a case before the rather short-sighted
Lord Redesdale in Dublin.

Collis had hardly begun his opening
remarks, before Lord Redesdale spoke
to him. 'Mr Collis, it is usual for
counsel to stand when they are
addressing us,' he said.

'But I am standing, my Lord,' Collis
insisted, 'on the bench.'

'Oh,' his Lordship went on, 'then Mr
Mahaffy, I must ask *you* to sit down
until your turn comes.'

'But I *am* sitting down, my Lord,' was
Mahaffy's swift response to the hapless
justice.

The celebrated American negro
minstrel, George Clarke, was being
harangued by a barrister in the closing
years of the last century when he
appeared as a witness in a court case.
'You are a minstrel by occupation?' the
lawyer sniffed.

'Yes, sir,' was the courteous reply.

'Isn't that a rather low calling?'

'I don't know if that's so, sir,' Clarke
said without any sign of annoyance, 'but

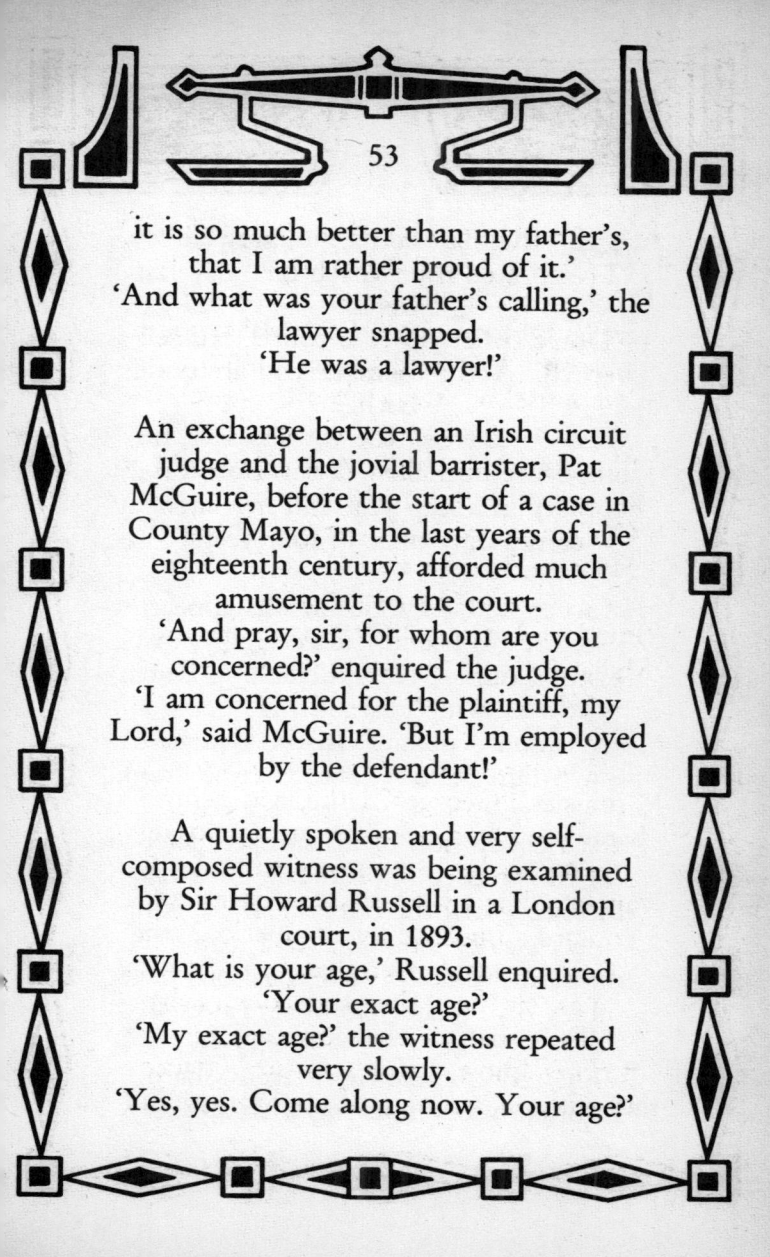

it is so much better than my father's,
that I am rather proud of it.'
'And what was your father's calling,' the
lawyer snapped.
'He was a lawyer!'

An exchange between an Irish circuit
judge and the jovial barrister, Pat
McGuire, before the start of a case in
County Mayo, in the last years of the
eighteenth century, afforded much
amusement to the court.
'And pray, sir, for whom are you
concerned?' enquired the judge.
'I am concerned for the plaintiff, my
Lord,' said McGuire. 'But I'm employed
by the defendant!'

A quietly spoken and very self-
composed witness was being examined
by Sir Howard Russell in a London
court, in 1893.
'What is your age,' Russell enquired.
'Your exact age?'
'My exact age?' the witness repeated
very slowly.
'Yes, yes. Come along now. Your age?'

'Well,' the man said again, very slowly, 'I celebrated my twelfth birthday last week.'

'Don't trifle with the court!' Russell warned. 'And remember you are under oath.'

'It is quite true,' the witness said, his composure unshaken. 'I was born on 29 February in a leap year and my birthday comes only once in four years!'

Attorney Timothy Coffin was appearing before his friend, Judge Colby, in Bristol County, USA, defending a man who was being charged with being a common drunkard. In the evidence against him, it was stated that he drank six glasses of liquor every day.

At the conclusion of his spirited defence of the accused, Coffin called for his discharge with the remark: 'If drinking six glasses a day makes a man a common drunkard, may the Lord have mercy on brother Colby and myself!'

The redoubtable barrister, Richard O'Brien, was discussing with an Irish

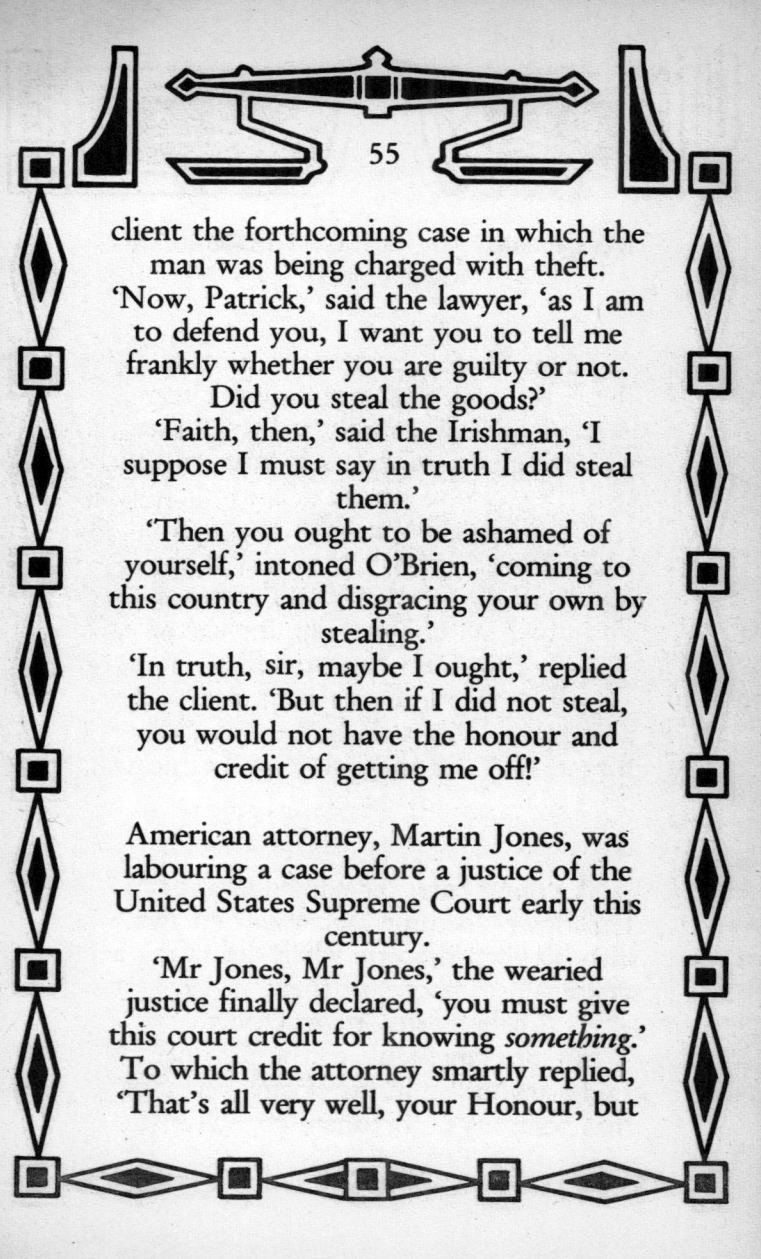

client the forthcoming case in which the
man was being charged with theft.

'Now, Patrick,' said the lawyer, 'as I am
to defend you, I want you to tell me
frankly whether you are guilty or not.
Did you steal the goods?'

'Faith, then,' said the Irishman, 'I
suppose I must say in truth I did steal
them.'

'Then you ought to be ashamed of
yourself,' intoned O'Brien, 'coming to
this country and disgracing your own by
stealing.'

'In truth, sir, maybe I ought,' replied
the client. 'But then if I did not steal,
you would not have the honour and
credit of getting me off!'

American attorney, Martin Jones, was
labouring a case before a justice of the
United States Supreme Court early this
century.

'Mr Jones, Mr Jones,' the wearied
justice finally declared, 'you must give
this court credit for knowing *something*.'
To which the attorney smartly replied,
'That's all very well, your Honour, but

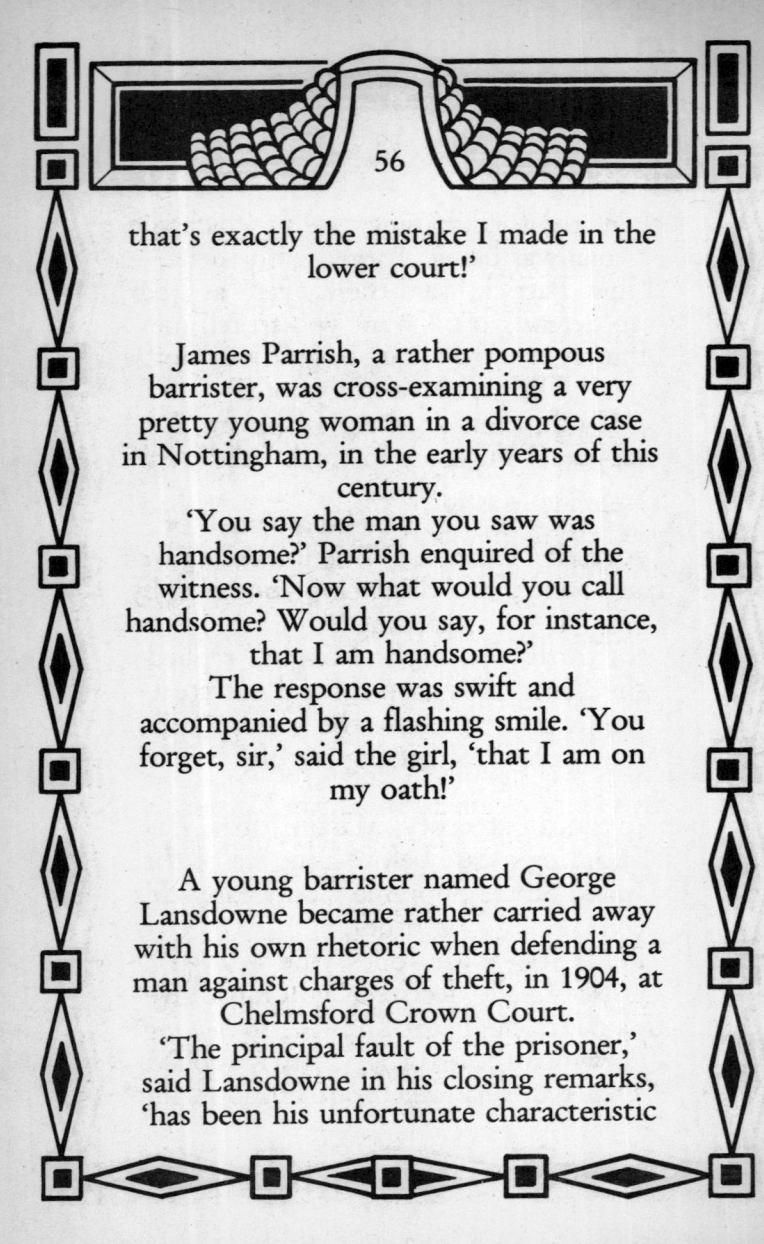

that's exactly the mistake I made in the lower court!'

James Parrish, a rather pompous barrister, was cross-examining a very pretty young woman in a divorce case in Nottingham, in the early years of this century.

'You say the man you saw was handsome?' Parrish enquired of the witness. 'Now what would you call handsome? Would you say, for instance, that I am handsome?'

The response was swift and accompanied by a flashing smile. 'You forget, sir,' said the girl, 'that I am on my oath!'

A young barrister named George Lansdowne became rather carried away with his own rhetoric when defending a man against charges of theft, in 1904, at Chelmsford Crown Court.

'The principal fault of the prisoner,' said Lansdowne in his closing remarks, 'has been his unfortunate characteristic

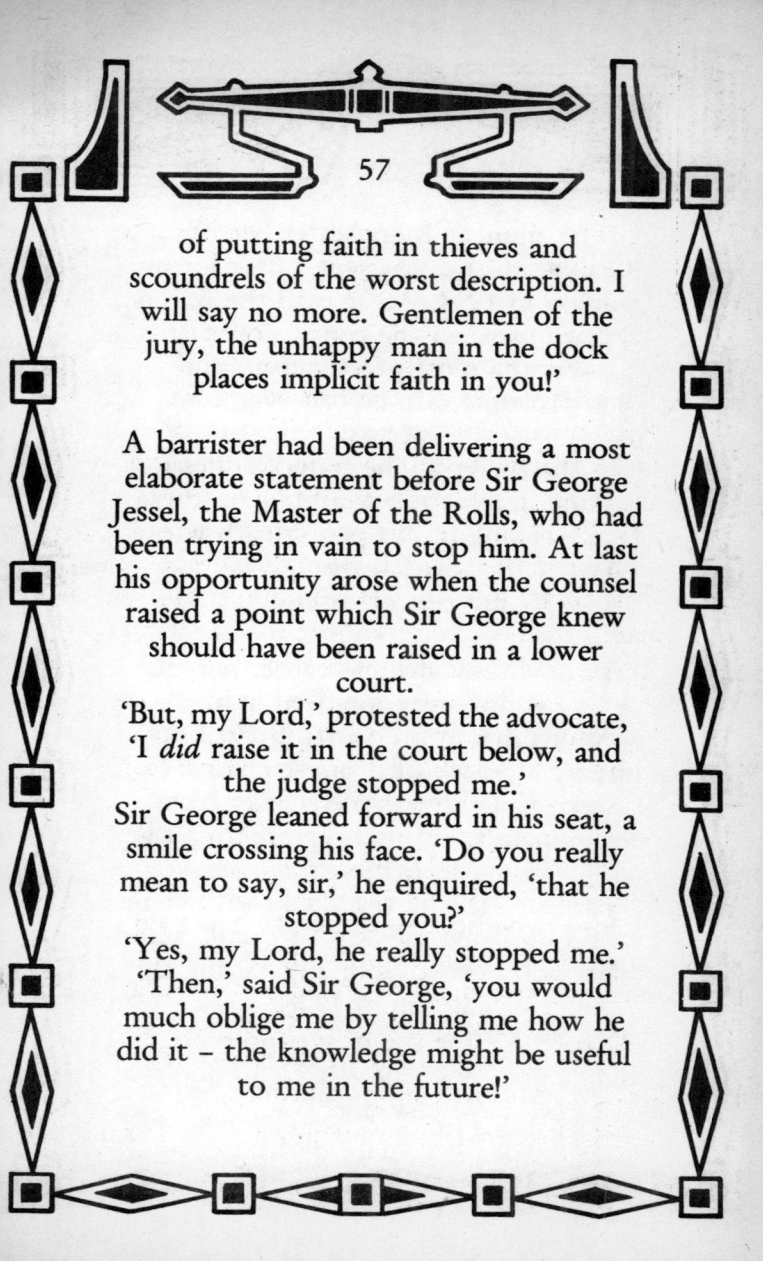

of putting faith in thieves and scoundrels of the worst description. I will say no more. Gentlemen of the jury, the unhappy man in the dock places implicit faith in you!'

A barrister had been delivering a most elaborate statement before Sir George Jessel, the Master of the Rolls, who had been trying in vain to stop him. At last his opportunity arose when the counsel raised a point which Sir George knew should have been raised in a lower court.

'But, my Lord,' protested the advocate, 'I *did* raise it in the court below, and the judge stopped me.'

Sir George leaned forward in his seat, a smile crossing his face. 'Do you really mean to say, sir,' he enquired, 'that he stopped you?'

'Yes, my Lord, he really stopped me.'

'Then,' said Sir George, 'you would much oblige me by telling me how he did it – the knowledge might be useful to me in the future!'

The eminent Manchester barrister, Claude Heath, was sent a case for his opinion in 1904. As he read the papers, Heath came to the conclusion that it was the most preposterous and improbable case he had ever come across.

On the final page he found a question asking if an action would *lie* on these facts. Taking up his pen, Heath wrote: 'Yes, if the witnesses would *lie*, too – but not otherwise!'

An obviously shy and rather nervous young man appeared in a Wolverhampton court, in 1912, to answer a breach of promise charge. For some time he was mercilessly cross-examined by counsel representing the young woman in the case.

'Now, sir,' the barrister said with some venom in his voice, 'am I to understand that you pressed your suit during the autumn of 1908?'

'No, sir,' came the quavering reply. 'I didn't press my suit at all – I bought a new one!'

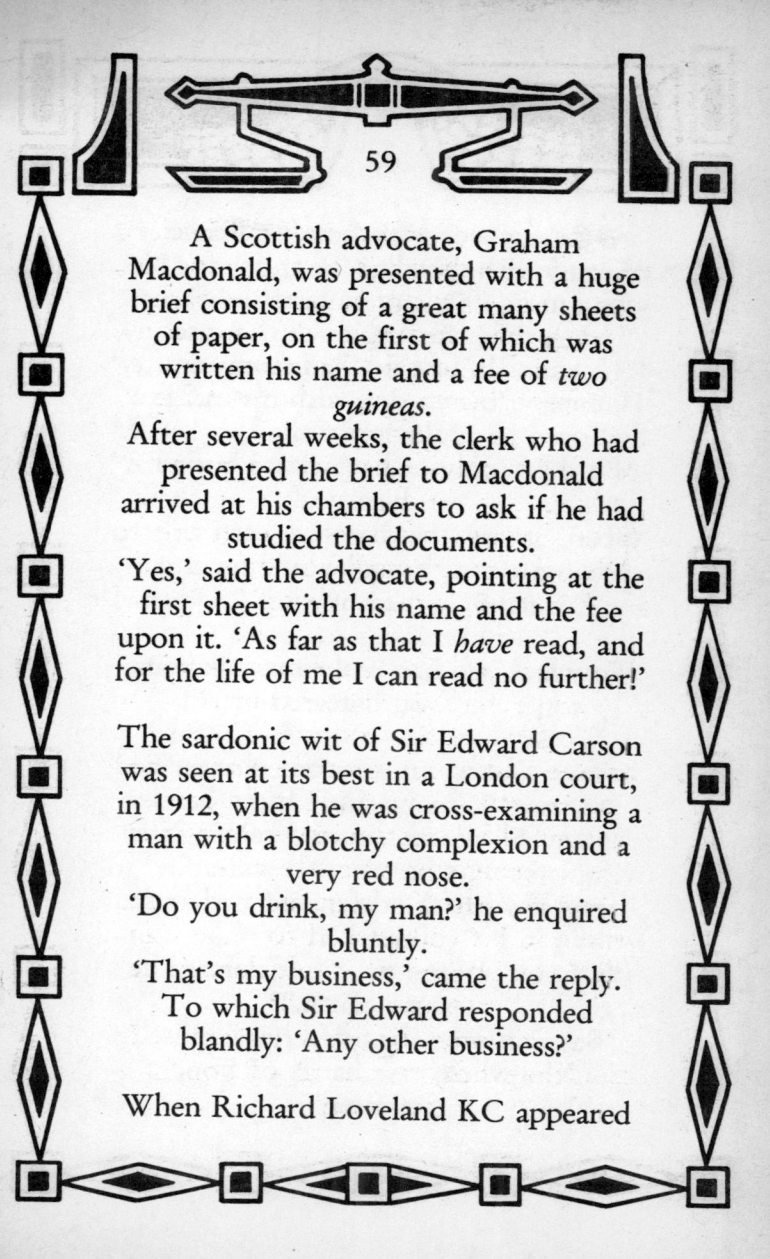

A Scottish advocate, Graham Macdonald, was presented with a huge brief consisting of a great many sheets of paper, on the first of which was written his name and a fee of *two guineas*.

After several weeks, the clerk who had presented the brief to Macdonald arrived at his chambers to ask if he had studied the documents.

'Yes,' said the advocate, pointing at the first sheet with his name and the fee upon it. 'As far as that I *have* read, and for the life of me I can read no further!'

The sardonic wit of Sir Edward Carson was seen at its best in a London court, in 1912, when he was cross-examining a man with a blotchy complexion and a very red nose.

'Do you drink, my man?' he enquired bluntly.

'That's my business,' came the reply.

To which Sir Edward responded blandly: 'Any other business?'

When Richard Loveland KC appeared

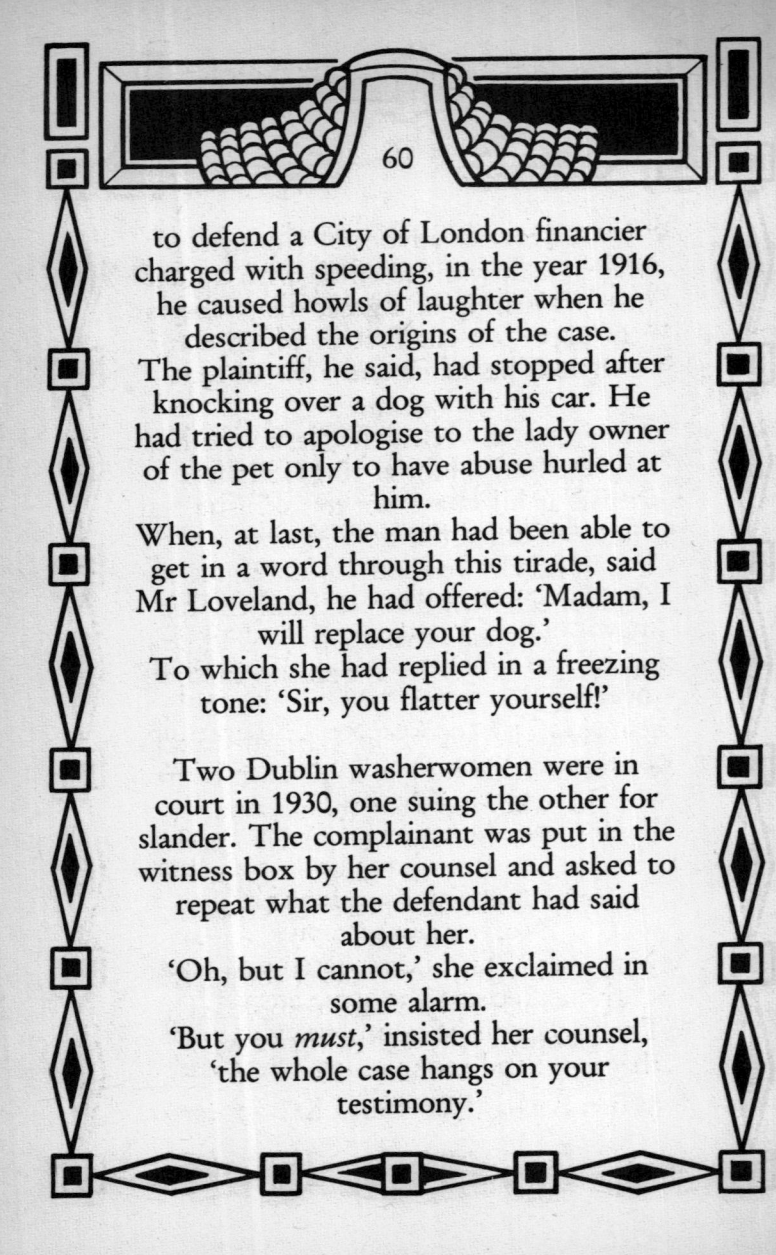

to defend a City of London financier
charged with speeding, in the year 1916,
he caused howls of laughter when he
described the origins of the case.

The plaintiff, he said, had stopped after
knocking over a dog with his car. He
had tried to apologise to the lady owner
of the pet only to have abuse hurled at
him.

When, at last, the man had been able to
get in a word through this tirade, said
Mr Loveland, he had offered: 'Madam, I
will replace your dog.'

To which she had replied in a freezing
tone: 'Sir, you flatter yourself!'

Two Dublin washerwomen were in
court in 1930, one suing the other for
slander. The complainant was put in the
witness box by her counsel and asked to
repeat what the defendant had said
about her.

'Oh, but I cannot,' she exclaimed in
some alarm.

'But you *must*,' insisted her counsel,
'the whole case hangs on your
testimony.'

'But it isn't fit for any decent person to hear,' the poor woman added.

'Well, in that case,' the helpful man of law suggested, 'just step up to the judge on the bench and whisper it in his ear.'

A poacher was up for trial before the magistrates in Bury St Edmunds, Suffolk, in 1936. The man had been caught complete with ferret, rabbit and net by a local gamekeeper.

Defence counsel alleged that the man knew nothing about the crime except that he had heard a noise and, climbing over a fence to see what it was, had been seized by the keeper. As the result of his convincing tale, the poacher was given a discharge.

'Excuse me,' he enquired of the bench as he was about to leave the stand, 'but can I be tried again for this?'

'No,' came the reply.

'Not ever again?' he repeated and was given precisely the same answer.

'Then will you be good enough to tell them to hand me over my ferret and my net?'

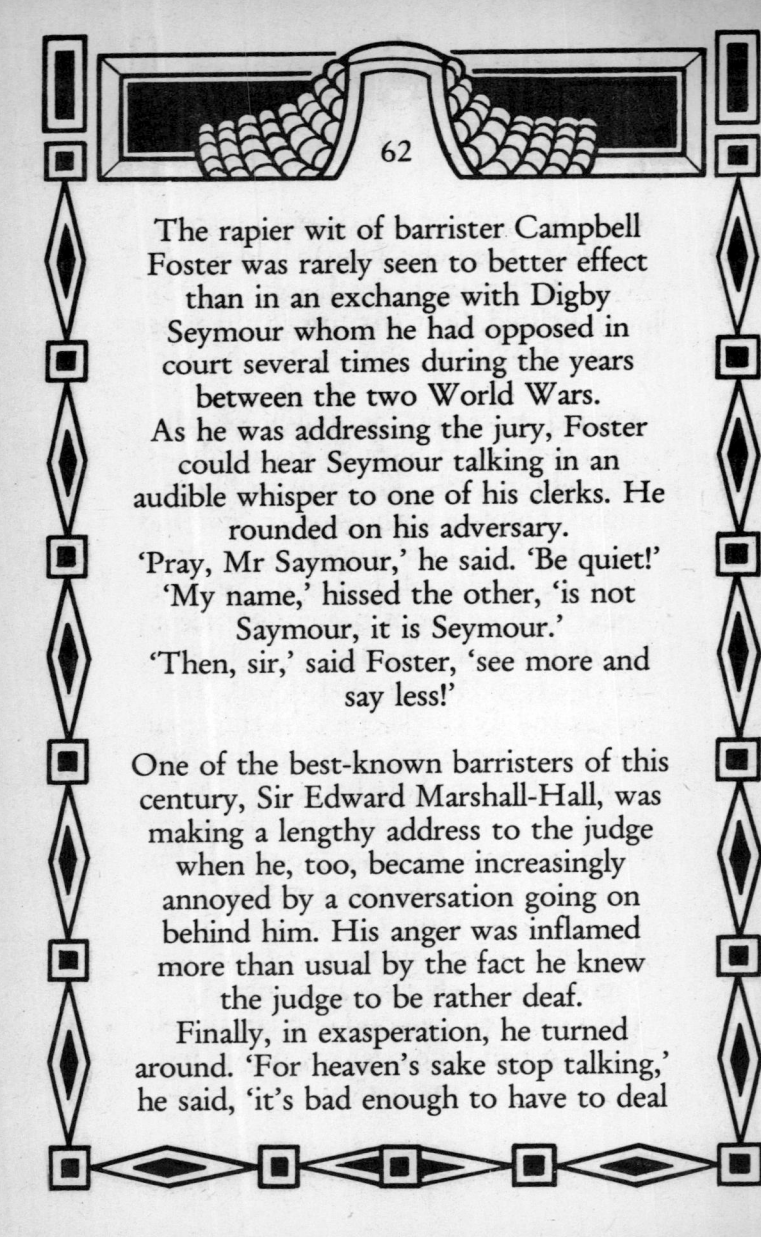

The rapier wit of barrister Campbell
Foster was rarely seen to better effect
than in an exchange with Digby
Seymour whom he had opposed in
court several times during the years
between the two World Wars.
As he was addressing the jury, Foster
could hear Seymour talking in an
audible whisper to one of his clerks. He
rounded on his adversary.
'Pray, Mr Saymour,' he said. 'Be quiet!'
'My name,' hissed the other, 'is not
Saymour, it is Seymour.'
'Then, sir,' said Foster, 'see more and
say less!'

One of the best-known barristers of this
century, Sir Edward Marshall-Hall, was
making a lengthy address to the judge
when he, too, became increasingly
annoyed by a conversation going on
behind him. His anger was inflamed
more than usual by the fact he knew
the judge to be rather deaf.
Finally, in exasperation, he turned
around. 'For heaven's sake stop talking,'
he said, 'it's bad enough to have to deal

with this deaf old man on the bench.'
The laughter which broke out even
caught the ear of the judge who held up
his hand for silence, and added: 'Hush,
please. I must get that on my notes.'

On another occasion, Marshall-Hall
asked a man who appeared far sharper
than he looked to give a definition of
absent-mindedness.
Shaking his head for a moment, the
man finally took a firm hold of the
witness box and replied, 'Well, I should
say that a man who thought he'd left
his watch at home and took it out of
his pocket to see if he had time to go
home to get it – I should say that that
chap was a little absent-minded!'

Barrister Oswald Cunningham was
examining an extremely cautious
witness in a case where a number of
valuable homing pigeons had been shot.
The witness was the owner of the
pigeons and a farmer by profession.
Deciding to play on the man's
nervousness, Cunningham asked: 'Are

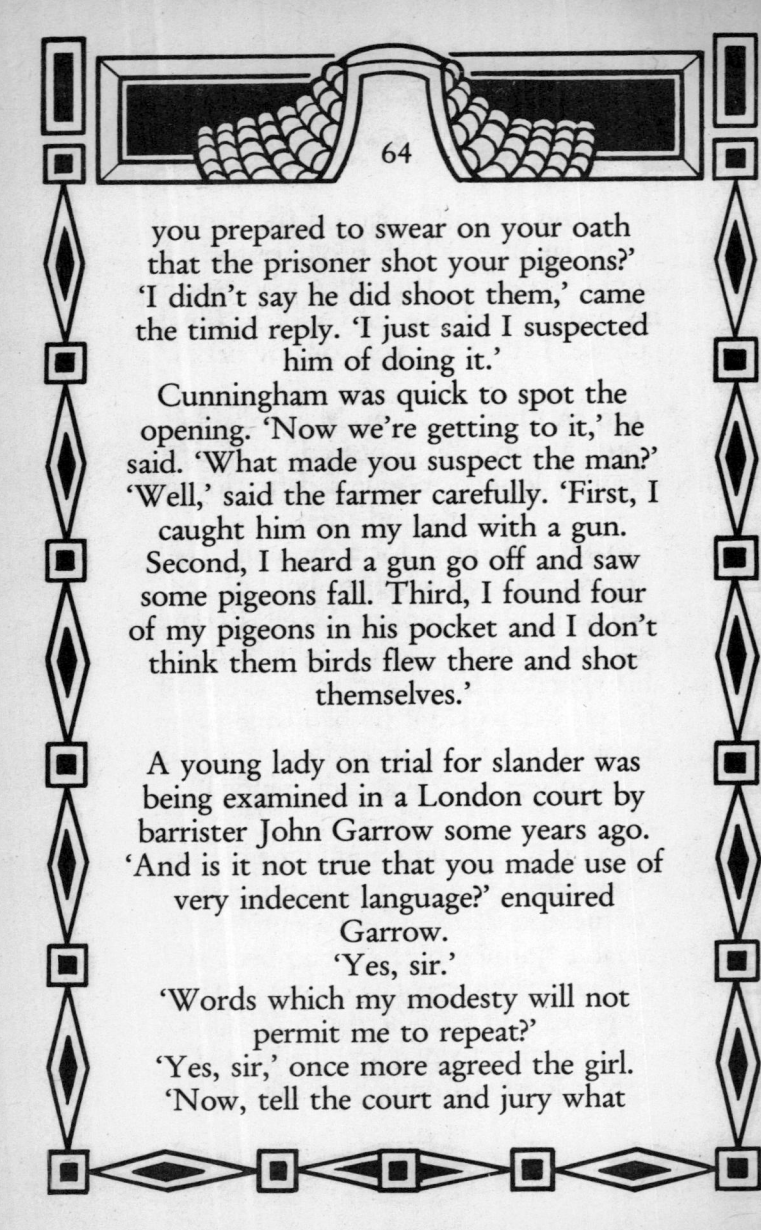

you prepared to swear on your oath that the prisoner shot your pigeons?' 'I didn't say he did shoot them,' came the timid reply. 'I just said I suspected him of doing it.'

Cunningham was quick to spot the opening. 'Now we're getting to it,' he said. 'What made you suspect the man?' 'Well,' said the farmer carefully. 'First, I caught him on my land with a gun. Second, I heard a gun go off and saw some pigeons fall. Third, I found four of my pigeons in his pocket and I don't think them birds flew there and shot themselves.'

A young lady on trial for slander was being examined in a London court by barrister John Garrow some years ago. 'And is it not true that you made use of very indecent language?' enquired Garrow.

'Yes, sir.'

'Words which my modesty will not permit me to repeat?'

'Yes, sir,' once more agreed the girl.

'Now, tell the court and jury what

those words were.'
'Sir,' the defendant replied, 'if *your modesty* will not permit you to express them, you cannot expect that *mine* will!'

The popular Sir David Williams was crossing the road to the Law Courts in London, in 1947, when a small boy stopped him.
'Please, sir,' said the lad addressing the imposing figure in his wig and gown, 'is this Chancery Lane?'
'It is,' replied Sir David, kindly.
'Ah, I knew it was,' exclaimed the boy.
'Then why did you bother to ask?'
'Because I wanted to have counsel's opinion for nothing!' the young rascal laughed before running off.

III

WITS in ERMINE

The Satire of Judges

The notorious Judge George Jeffreys, famed for his brutal sentences, could also be hard with the lawyers who appeared before him. In 1684, he was confronted one morning by the quick-witted Richard Baxter whom he had encountered several times before – usually coming off second best.

'Richard,' he declared, determined to best the other man for once. 'I see a rogue in your face.'

Before the judge could even grin, Baxter replied. 'I did not know,' he said, 'that my face was a mirror!'

A simple Norfolk countryman was giving evidence in a dispute over a piece of land not far from where he lived.

At one juncture during the cross-examination, the judge interrupted to ask the man: 'What do you call that water which runs on the south side of the field?'

To which the countryman replied without the slightest change of expression, 'My Lord, our water comes without calling.'

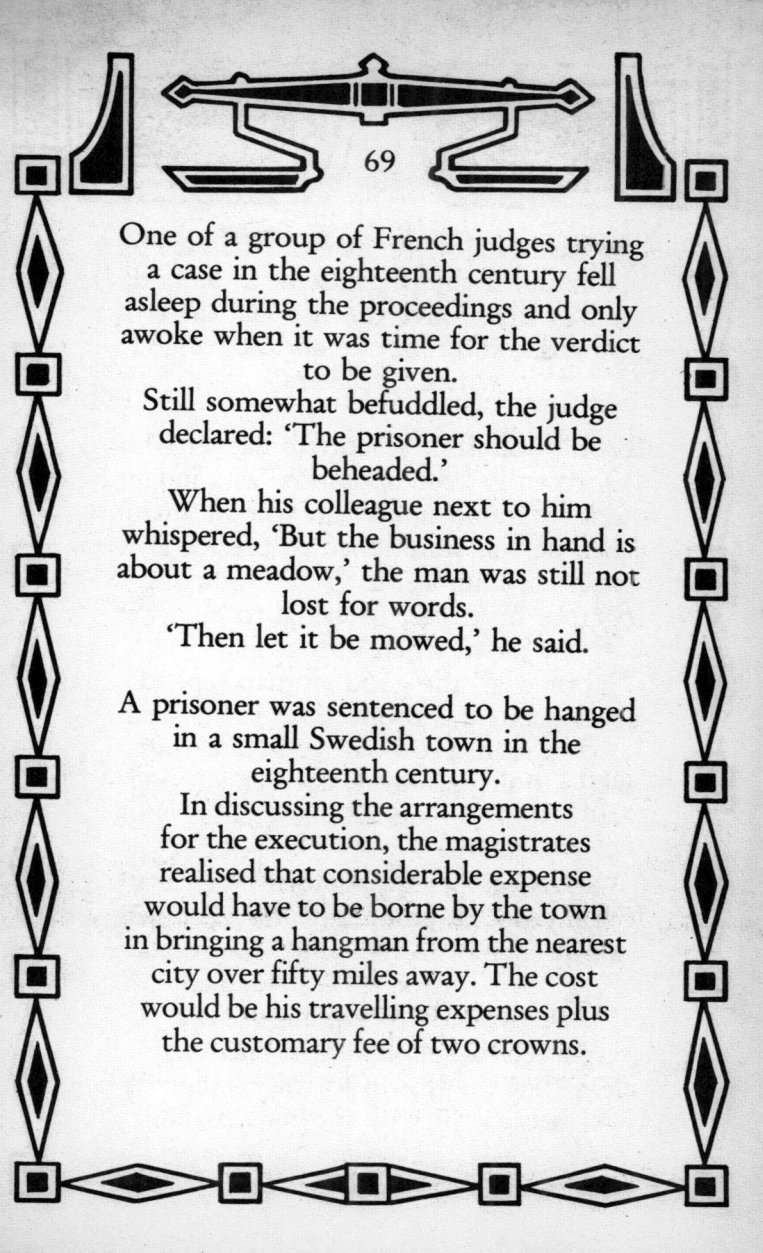

One of a group of French judges trying a case in the eighteenth century fell asleep during the proceedings and only awoke when it was time for the verdict to be given.

Still somewhat befuddled, the judge declared: 'The prisoner should be beheaded.'

When his colleague next to him whispered, 'But the business in hand is about a meadow,' the man was still not lost for words.

'Then let it be mowed,' he said.

A prisoner was sentenced to be hanged in a small Swedish town in the eighteenth century.

In discussing the arrangements for the execution, the magistrates realised that considerable expense would have to be borne by the town in bringing a hangman from the nearest city over fifty miles away. The cost would be his travelling expenses plus the customary fee of two crowns.

At this, one of the men on the bench spoke up. 'I think, gentlemen,' he said, 'we had better give the criminal the two crowns and let him go and be hanged where he pleases!'

Robbie Johnson, a Scottish farmer who had recently been appointed as a judge, suddenly found himself in a predicament when he was summoned to preside at a court in Dundee, in 1769. Gathering together his robes, he called to his wife: 'Janet, where's my wig?'
'Your wig?' the good woman replied coming into his room. 'Did I ever hear such a man! How can you have your wig? Don't you know the hen's laying in it?'

A short-tempered, eighteenth-century Welsh judge summoned to his chambers a carpenter who had failed to erect a gibbet in time for a scheduled execution. Before going in, the carpenter had explained to the judge's clerk that the reason for his negligence was because he had not been paid for

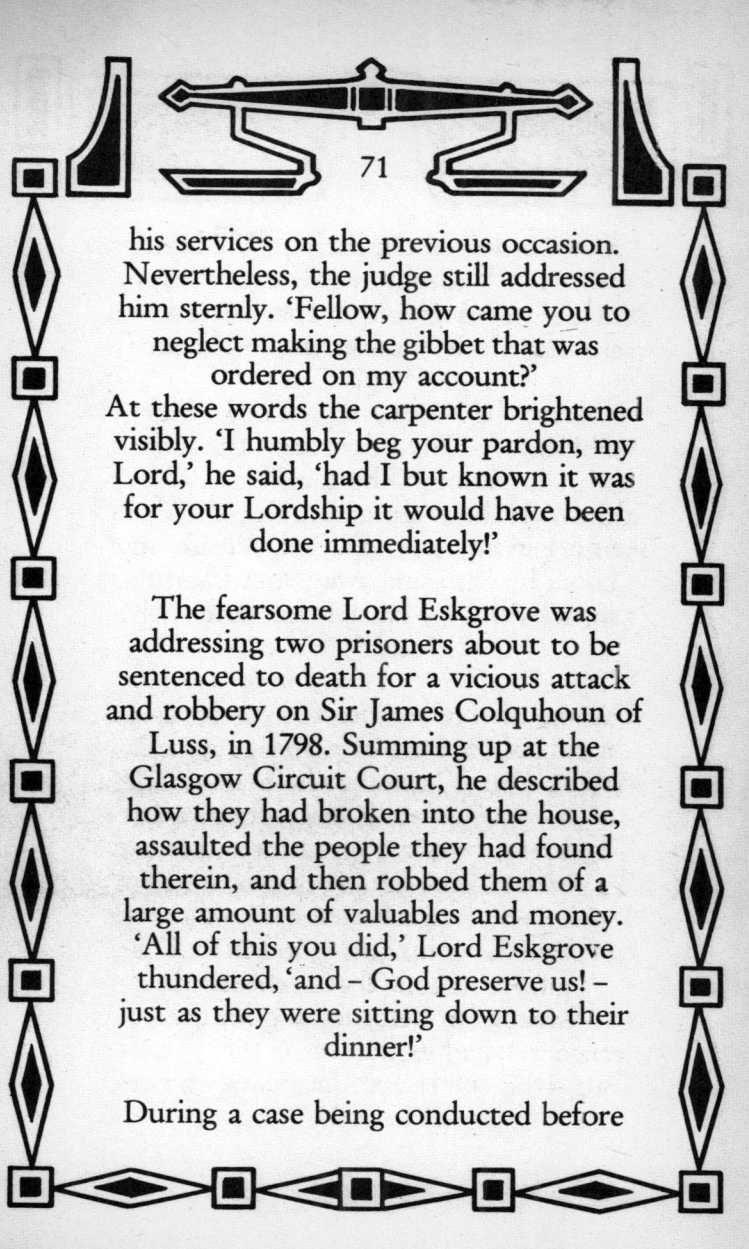

his services on the previous occasion.
Nevertheless, the judge still addressed
him sternly. 'Fellow, how came you to
neglect making the gibbet that was
ordered on my account?'
At these words the carpenter brightened
visibly. 'I humbly beg your pardon, my
Lord,' he said, 'had I but known it was
for your Lordship it would have been
done immediately!'

The fearsome Lord Eskgrove was
addressing two prisoners about to be
sentenced to death for a vicious attack
and robbery on Sir James Colquhoun of
Luss, in 1798. Summing up at the
Glasgow Circuit Court, he described
how they had broken into the house,
assaulted the people they had found
therein, and then robbed them of a
large amount of valuables and money.
'All of this you did,' Lord Eskgrove
thundered, 'and – God preserve us! –
just as they were sitting down to their
dinner!'

During a case being conducted before

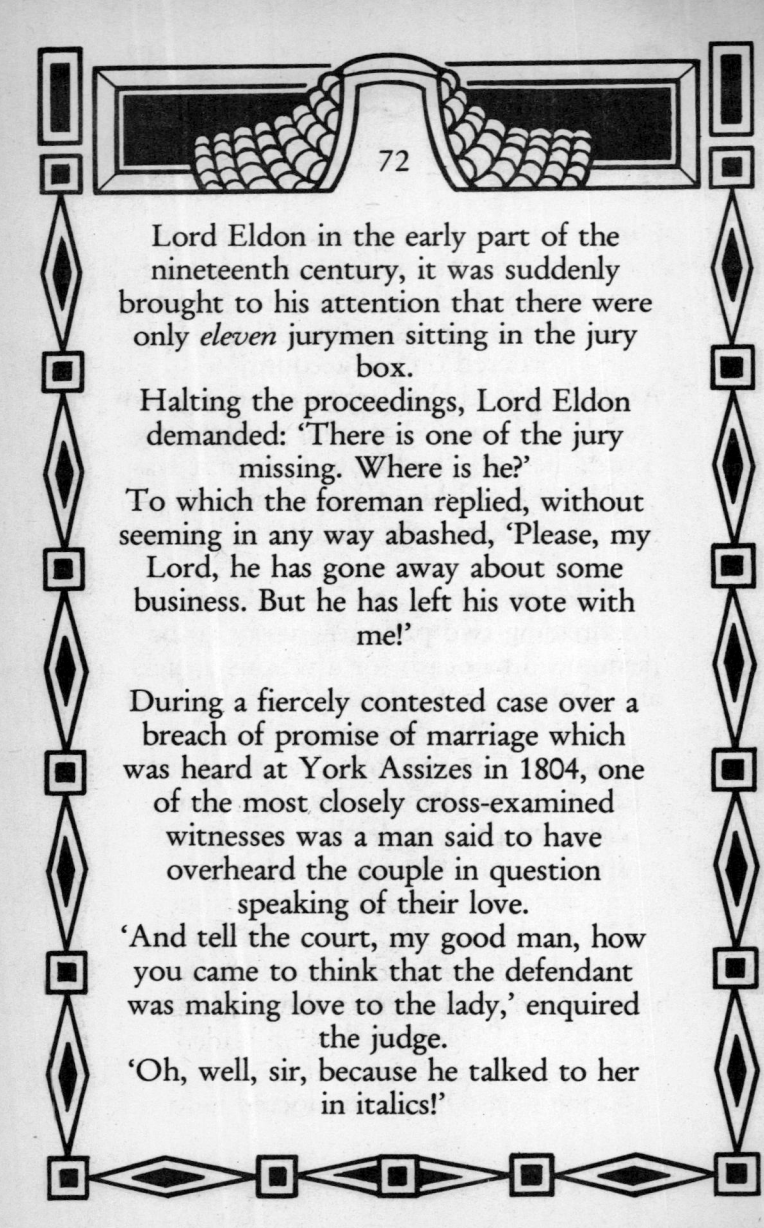

Lord Eldon in the early part of the nineteenth century, it was suddenly brought to his attention that there were only *eleven* jurymen sitting in the jury box.

Halting the proceedings, Lord Eldon demanded: 'There is one of the jury missing. Where is he?'

To which the foreman replied, without seeming in any way abashed, 'Please, my Lord, he has gone away about some business. But he has left his vote with me!'

During a fiercely contested case over a breach of promise of marriage which was heard at York Assizes in 1804, one of the most closely cross-examined witnesses was a man said to have overheard the couple in question speaking of their love.

'And tell the court, my good man, how you came to think that the defendant was making love to the lady,' enquired the judge.

'Oh, well, sir, because he talked to her in italics!'

Daniel Boyd, a well-known Irish judge, who had something of a reputation as a drunkard and used to conceal a cup of brandy in the ink-well of his desk, from which he would take sips through his quill pen, was hearing a case of a man charged with being drunk and disorderly.

After the case had been prolonged longer than Judge Boyd could stand, he interrupted the proceedings and demanded of the accused:

'Come now, my good man, let's have no more prevaricating. Tell the truth: were you drunk or were you sober on this occasion?'

For a moment, the man was taken aback. Then, looking significantly at the ink-well and quill pen, he said, 'Oh, quite sober, my Lord. As sober as a judge!'

An Irishman being tried for bigamy before Lord Cockburn at the Justiciary Court in Glasgow, in 1845, pleaded guilty to the charge and thereby forfeited the right to speak in his

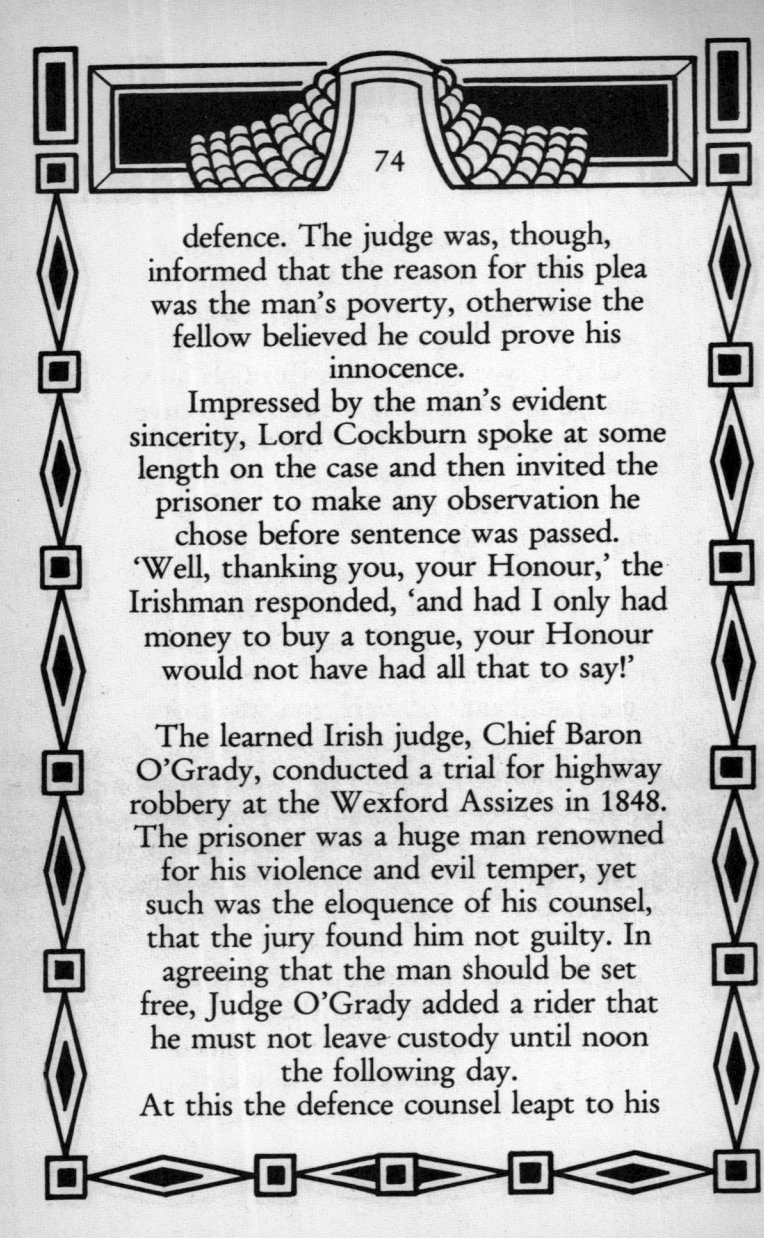

defence. The judge was, though, informed that the reason for this plea was the man's poverty, otherwise the fellow believed he could prove his innocence.

Impressed by the man's evident sincerity, Lord Cockburn spoke at some length on the case and then invited the prisoner to make any observation he chose before sentence was passed.

'Well, thanking you, your Honour,' the Irishman responded, 'and had I only had money to buy a tongue, your Honour would not have had all that to say!'

The learned Irish judge, Chief Baron O'Grady, conducted a trial for highway robbery at the Wexford Assizes in 1848. The prisoner was a huge man renowned for his violence and evil temper, yet such was the eloquence of his counsel, that the jury found him not guilty. In agreeing that the man should be set free, Judge O'Grady added a rider that he must not leave custody until noon the following day.

At this the defence counsel leapt to his

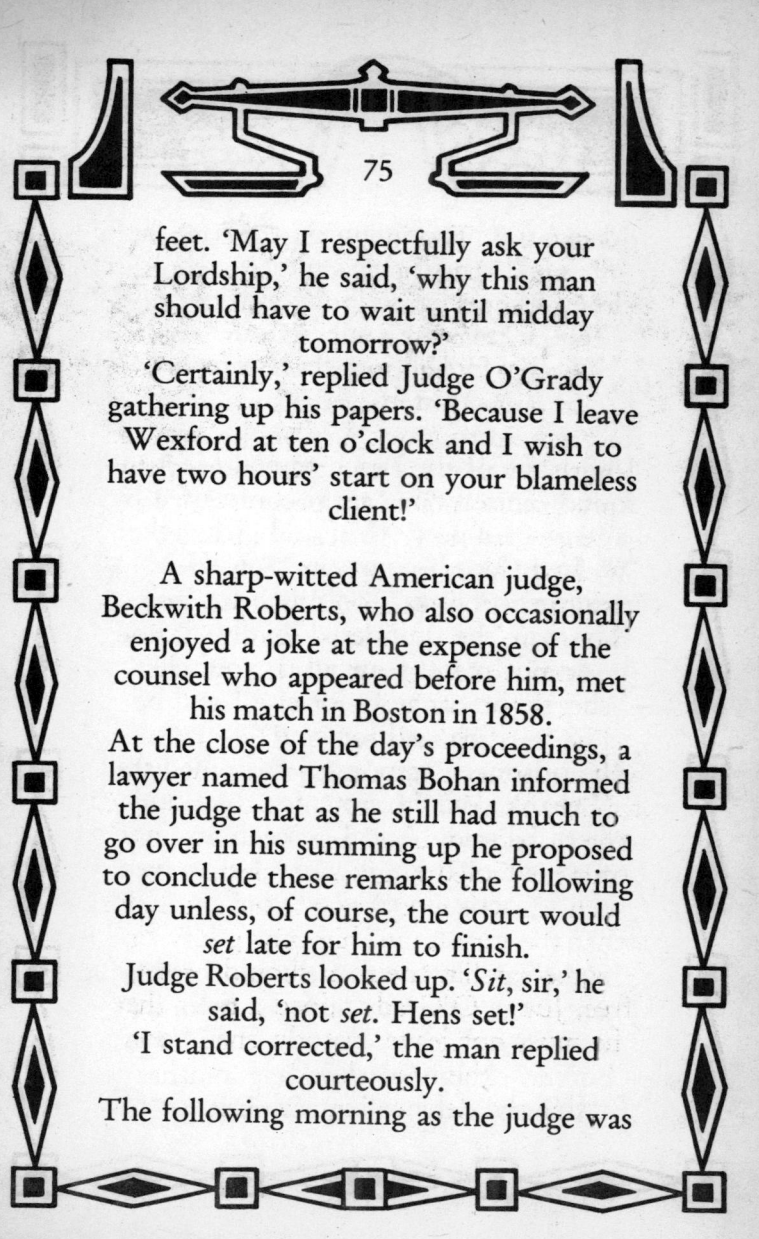

feet. 'May I respectfully ask your Lordship,' he said, 'why this man should have to wait until midday tomorrow?'

'Certainly,' replied Judge O'Grady gathering up his papers. 'Because I leave Wexford at ten o'clock and I wish to have two hours' start on your blameless client!'

A sharp-witted American judge, Beckwith Roberts, who also occasionally enjoyed a joke at the expense of the counsel who appeared before him, met his match in Boston in 1858.

At the close of the day's proceedings, a lawyer named Thomas Bohan informed the judge that as he still had much to go over in his summing up he proposed to conclude these remarks the following day unless, of course, the court would *set* late for him to finish.

Judge Roberts looked up. '*Sit*, sir,' he said, 'not *set*. Hens set!'

'I stand corrected,' the man replied courteously.

The following morning as the judge was

delivering his opinion on the case, he said, 'And I think under such circumstances an action would not *lay*.' '*Lie*, if it please your honour,' said Thomas Bohan in a flash, 'not *lay*. Hens *lay*!'

A Justice of the Peace named Morgan found himself once again confronted by a renowned petty thief and pickpocket in a Cardiff court, in 1866. His exasperation was too much for him. 'My man,' he thundered loudly, 'if you do not mend your ways, you will shortly be hanged – or else I will be hanged for you!' The prisoner's response was immediate. 'I thank your Honour for that kind offer,' he said. 'And I beseech you not to be out of the way when I shall have occasion to need you!'

In the middle years of the nineteenth century, a man was brought before a court in Arkansas, close to the Texas border, charged with killing another man and stealing his mule.

At the end of the proceedings, Judge Hughes announced that because of the particular location of the crime, the prisoner could opt to be sentenced under either Texas law or Arkansas law. The man chose Arkansas law.

'Then I discharge you on the count of stealing the mule,' said Judge Hughes, 'and sentence you to hang for killing the man.'

The prisoner immediately turned white. 'Oh, please judge,' he said, 'I would rather have the Texas law.'

Judge Hughes shrugged his shoulders. 'All right. Under the law of Texas I fine you for killing the man and hang you for stealing the mule!'

In a police court in County Tyrone in 1860, the magistrate was just about to pass sentence on a man found guilty of the theft of some livestock, when there was a sudden uproar from the prisoner in the dock.

'Are you going to condemn me on the oath of those two witnesses?' he demanded of the man on the bench.

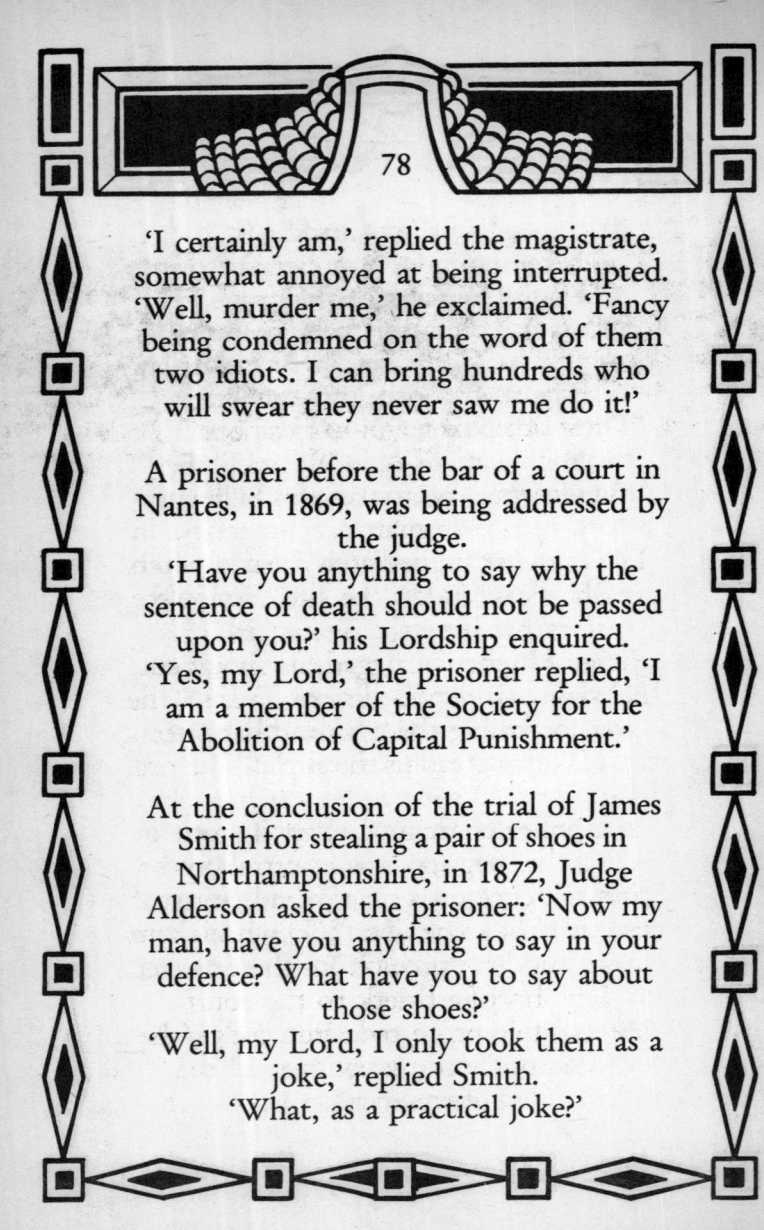

'I certainly am,' replied the magistrate, somewhat annoyed at being interrupted. 'Well, murder me,' he exclaimed. 'Fancy being condemned on the word of them two idiots. I can bring hundreds who will swear they never saw me do it!'

A prisoner before the bar of a court in Nantes, in 1869, was being addressed by the judge.
'Have you anything to say why the sentence of death should not be passed upon you?' his Lordship enquired.
'Yes, my Lord,' the prisoner replied, 'I am a member of the Society for the Abolition of Capital Punishment.'

At the conclusion of the trial of James Smith for stealing a pair of shoes in Northamptonshire, in 1872, Judge Alderson asked the prisoner: 'Now my man, have you anything to say in your defence? What have you to say about those shoes?'
'Well, my Lord, I only took them as a joke,' replied Smith.
'What, as a practical joke?'

'Yes, my Lord.'
'And how far did you carry them?'
enquired Judge Alderson.
'About a mile and a half, my Lord.'
'I think,' said the judge, 'that is carrying
the joke too far. Three months
imprisonment and hard labour!'

A notorious hell-raiser was brought
before Judge Ames in San Francisco, in
1876. The man had been arrested after
smashing up a brothel – but there were
fears that because of the lack of
witnesses prepared to speak up against
the rowdy he would get off. Indeed, the
man, from New England, had beaten
charges against him several times before.
However, as soon as he was brought
into court, Judge Ames broke into a
tirade of abuse. 'You lantern-jawed
Yankee cuss, we've caught you at last,
have we?' he exploded. 'I'll commit you
at once.'
The horrified clerk to the court
immediately protested. 'But, judge,' he
whispered, 'you must hear all the
evidence.'

'Evidence be blowed,' the judge roared. 'Wasn't I there and didn't I see it all for myself?'

The puckish sense of humour possessed by Judge Bampton was evident even from his earliest days as a country lawyer. One day, in 1876, he was arguing a case before a rather snappy old magistrate in Suffolk, who informed him very peremptorily that 'two blacks do not make a white'.

'They may sometimes,' Bampton replied instantly.

'Indeed?' said the old man, with a touch of disagreeableness in his voice. 'And how so?'

'A pair of black Spanish fowls may be the parents of a white egg,' he said without hesitation.

A meek-looking farm labourer appeared before Essex magistrates in 1879, charged with stealing six chickens from a Mr Jones.

'And you say you are innocent of the charge?' enquired the magistrate.

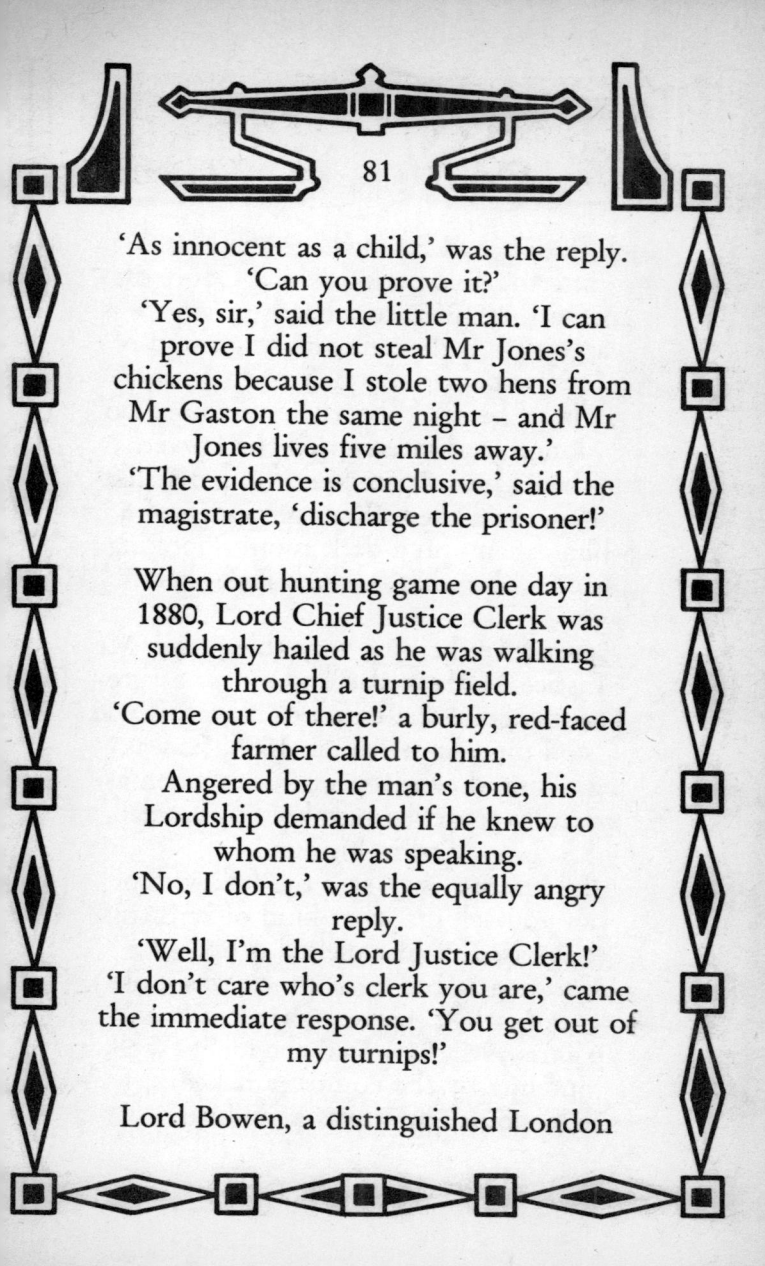

'As innocent as a child,' was the reply.
'Can you prove it?'

'Yes, sir,' said the little man. 'I can prove I did not steal Mr Jones's chickens because I stole two hens from Mr Gaston the same night – and Mr Jones lives five miles away.'

'The evidence is conclusive,' said the magistrate, 'discharge the prisoner!'

When out hunting game one day in 1880, Lord Chief Justice Clerk was suddenly hailed as he was walking through a turnip field.

'Come out of there!' a burly, red-faced farmer called to him.

Angered by the man's tone, his Lordship demanded if he knew to whom he was speaking.

'No, I don't,' was the equally angry reply.

'Well, I'm the Lord Justice Clerk!'

'I don't care who's clerk you are,' came the immediate response. 'You get out of my turnips!'

Lord Bowen, a distinguished London

judge, had listened for an almost interminable period in the Court of Appeal, in 1883, to a barrister who was arguing a bad point on the ground of there being an equity in the case. Finally, he could bear the discourse no longer and interrupted the lawyer. 'When I hear of an equity in a case like this,' he sighed, 'I am reminded of a blind man – in a dark room – looking for a black hat – which isn't there!'

Apart from being a very able judge, Mr Justice Mathew also had a very astute knowledge of the tricks of criminals and con men. One day, in 1884, he was walking down Regent Street when a man approached him holding a small bird in his hand.

'Excuse me, sir,' said the fellow, 'but can you tell me what kind of bird this is? I've just picked it up.'

Looking at the bird, which was quite evidently a sparrow that had been painted, Mathew told the man, 'Well, judging by the company it keeps, I should say it was a jail-bird.'

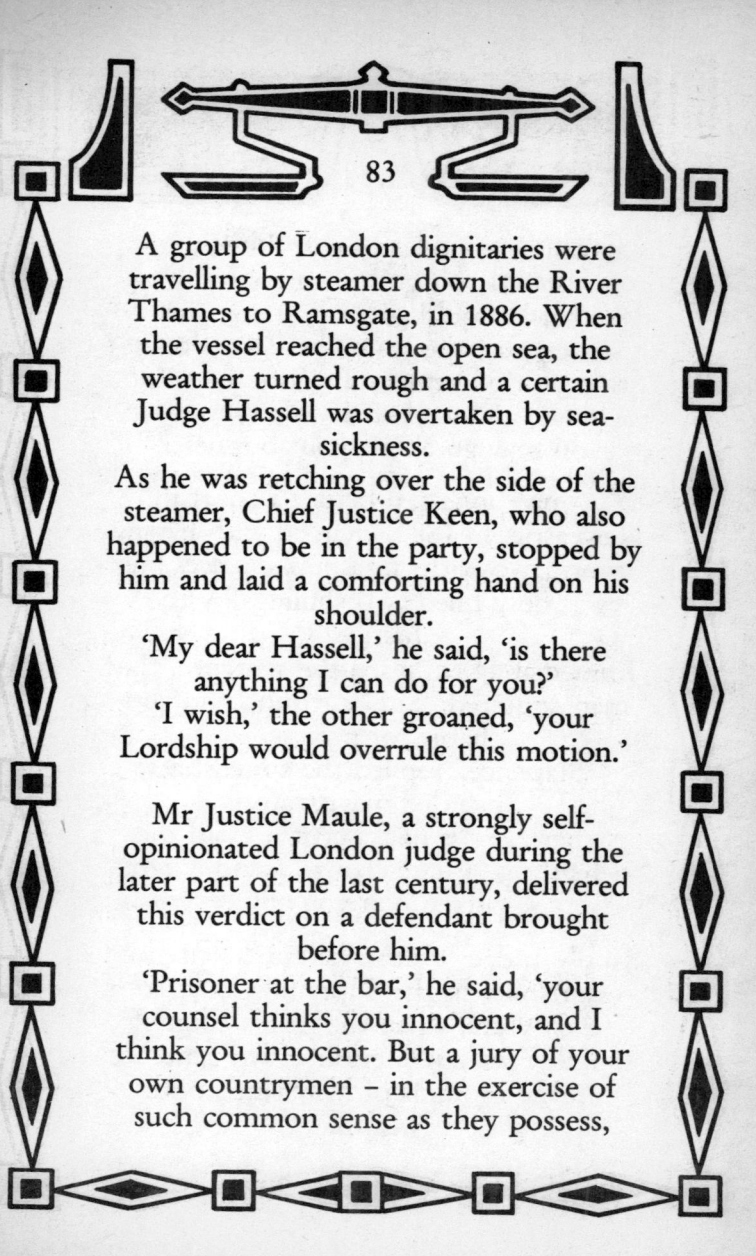

A group of London dignitaries were
travelling by steamer down the River
Thames to Ramsgate, in 1886. When
the vessel reached the open sea, the
weather turned rough and a certain
Judge Hassell was overtaken by sea-
sickness.

As he was retching over the side of the
steamer, Chief Justice Keen, who also
happened to be in the party, stopped by
him and laid a comforting hand on his
shoulder.

'My dear Hassell,' he said, 'is there
anything I can do for you?'

'I wish,' the other groaned, 'your
Lordship would overrule this motion.'

Mr Justice Maule, a strongly self-
opinionated London judge during the
later part of the last century, delivered
this verdict on a defendant brought
before him.

'Prisoner at the bar,' he said, 'your
counsel thinks you innocent, and I
think you innocent. But a jury of your
own countrymen – in the exercise of
such common sense as they possess,

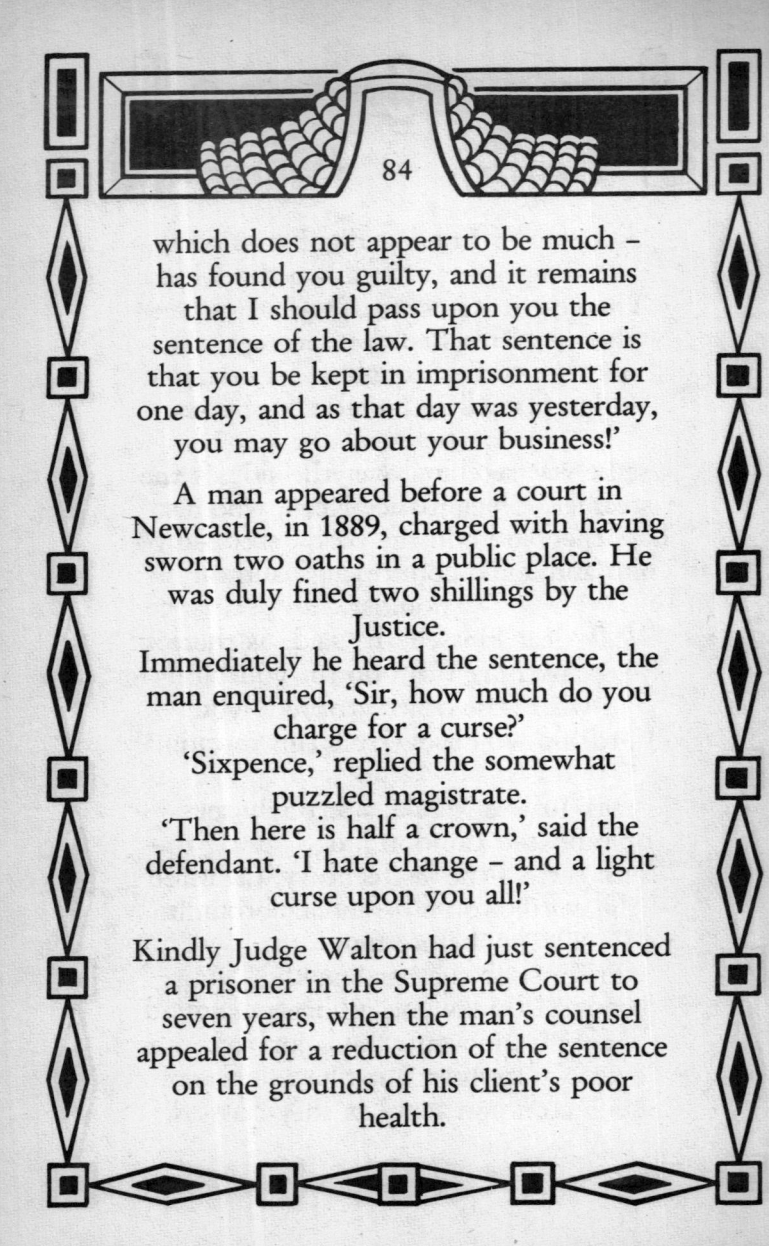

which does not appear to be much –
has found you guilty, and it remains
that I should pass upon you the
sentence of the law. That sentence is
that you be kept in imprisonment for
one day, and as that day was yesterday,
you may go about your business!'

A man appeared before a court in
Newcastle, in 1889, charged with having
sworn two oaths in a public place. He
was duly fined two shillings by the
Justice.
Immediately he heard the sentence, the
man enquired, 'Sir, how much do you
charge for a curse?'
'Sixpence,' replied the somewhat
puzzled magistrate.
'Then here is half a crown,' said the
defendant. 'I hate change – and a light
curse upon you all!'

Kindly Judge Walton had just sentenced
a prisoner in the Supreme Court to
seven years, when the man's counsel
appealed for a reduction of the sentence
on the grounds of his client's poor
health.

'Your Lordship,' the lawyer said, 'I believe that my client will be unable to live out half that term, and I beg you to change the sentence.'

Judge Walton pondered for a moment and then replied: 'Well, under those circumstances, I will change the sentence. I will make it for life instead of seven years.'

NB The original sentence stood.

Sir Peter O'Brien, a Lord Chief Justice of Ireland in the 1890s, had a reputation for being swayed by evidence given by pretty witnesses. And so while presenting a particularly hopeless case, a lawyer named Denis Kelly put a blushing young girl into the witness box.

For a few moments Sir Peter was quite distracted by the beauty before him, but catching sight of the look on lawyer Kelly's face, he said:

'Mr Kelly this will not do. I don't mind admitting there may have been occasions when testimony of this kind might have affected me, but that is a

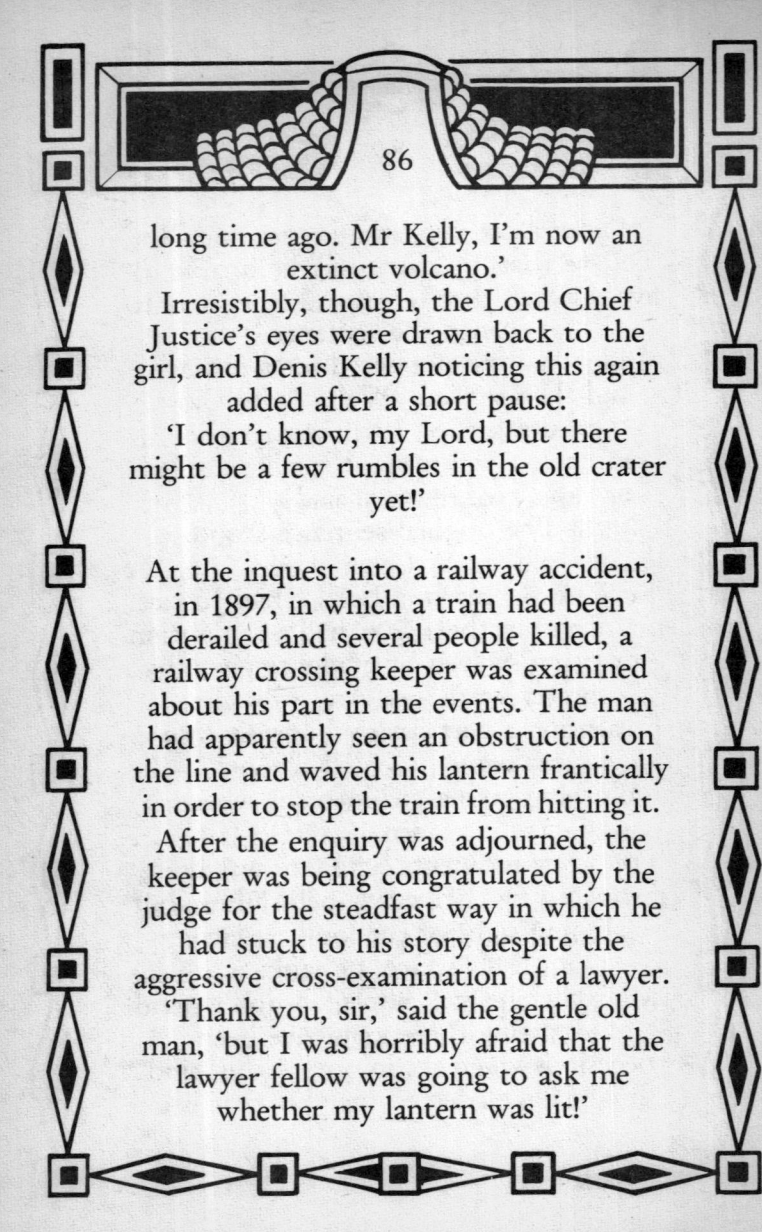

long time ago. Mr Kelly, I'm now an
extinct volcano.'
Irresistibly, though, the Lord Chief
Justice's eyes were drawn back to the
girl, and Denis Kelly noticing this again
added after a short pause:
'I don't know, my Lord, but there
might be a few rumbles in the old crater
yet!'

At the inquest into a railway accident,
in 1897, in which a train had been
derailed and several people killed, a
railway crossing keeper was examined
about his part in the events. The man
had apparently seen an obstruction on
the line and waved his lantern frantically
in order to stop the train from hitting it.
After the enquiry was adjourned, the
keeper was being congratulated by the
judge for the steadfast way in which he
had stuck to his story despite the
aggressive cross-examination of a lawyer.
'Thank you, sir,' said the gentle old
man, 'but I was horribly afraid that the
lawyer fellow was going to ask me
whether my lantern was lit!'

A conceited Liverpool judge, William Huddlestone, and his advocate friend, Judge Paul Manisty, were dining with the Lord Mayor in 1897. At the appropriate moment, the Lord Mayor proposed the Queen's health and Manisty stood up with him to raise his glass.

At this, Judge Huddlestone seized his colleague's sleeve and pulled him down, saying, 'Sit down, you damned fool. We *are* the Queen!'

On a hot summer day, in 1898, Judge Bampton found himself growing increasingly impatient with the long-winded manner in which certain details of the case he was hearing were being presented by one of the counsels before him. Yet unable to do anything to prevent the flow of words, he finally found an outlet for his frustration by scribbling the following lines on a piece of paper which he passed to the clerk of the court sitting below him:

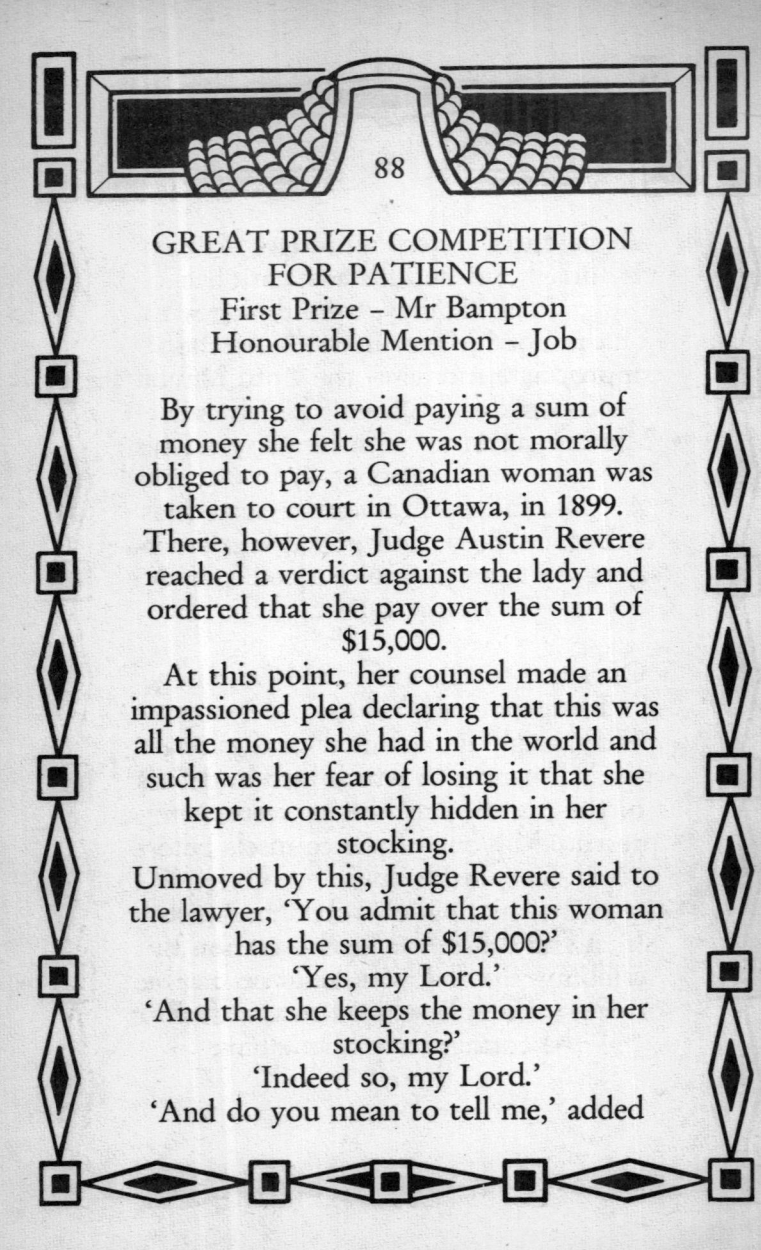

GREAT PRIZE COMPETITION FOR PATIENCE
First Prize – Mr Bampton
Honourable Mention – Job

By trying to avoid paying a sum of money she felt she was not morally obliged to pay, a Canadian woman was taken to court in Ottawa, in 1899. There, however, Judge Austin Revere reached a verdict against the lady and ordered that she pay over the sum of $15,000.

At this point, her counsel made an impassioned plea declaring that this was all the money she had in the world and such was her fear of losing it that she kept it constantly hidden in her stocking.

Unmoved by this, Judge Revere said to the lawyer, 'You admit that this woman has the sum of $15,000?'

'Yes, my Lord.'

'And that she keeps the money in her stocking?'

'Indeed so, my Lord.'

'And do you mean to tell me,' added

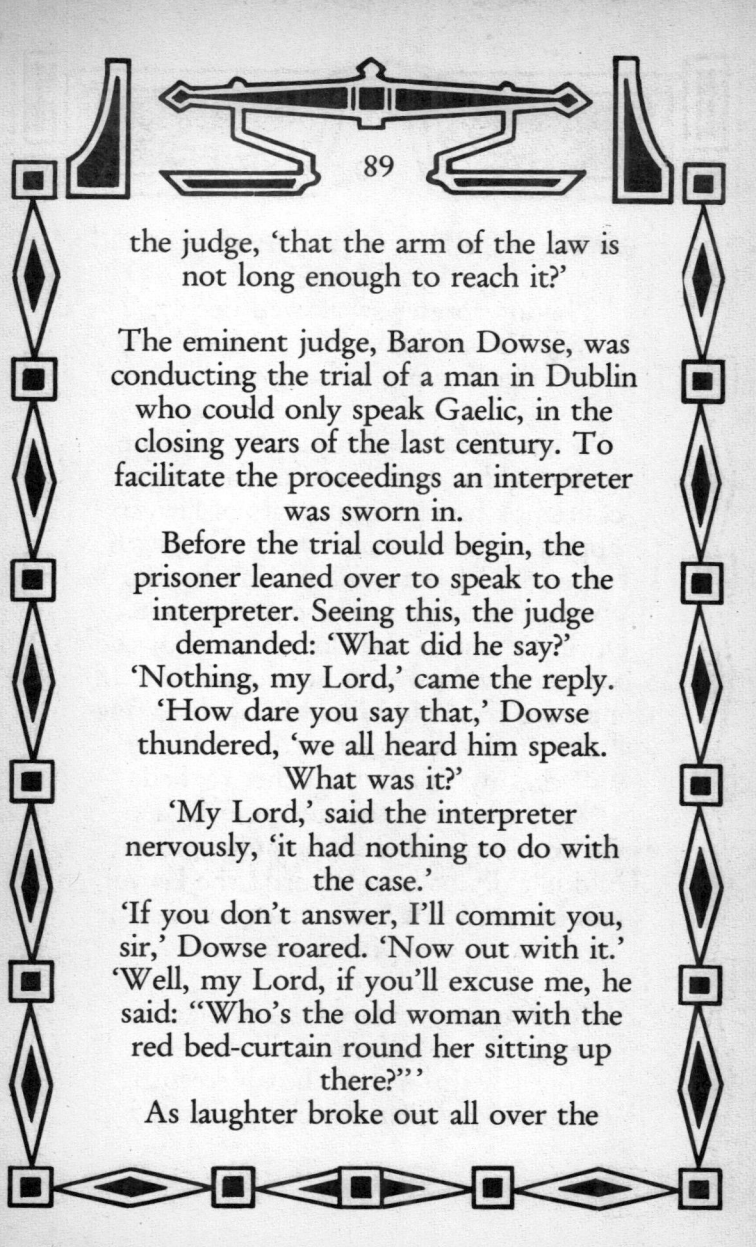

the judge, 'that the arm of the law is not long enough to reach it?'

The eminent judge, Baron Dowse, was conducting the trial of a man in Dublin who could only speak Gaelic, in the closing years of the last century. To facilitate the proceedings an interpreter was sworn in.

Before the trial could begin, the prisoner leaned over to speak to the interpreter. Seeing this, the judge demanded: 'What did he say?'

'Nothing, my Lord,' came the reply.

'How dare you say that,' Dowse thundered, 'we all heard him speak. What was it?'

'My Lord,' said the interpreter nervously, 'it had nothing to do with the case.'

'If you don't answer, I'll commit you, sir,' Dowse roared. 'Now out with it.'

'Well, my Lord, if you'll excuse me, he said: "Who's the old woman with the red bed-curtain round her sitting up there?"'

As laughter broke out all over the

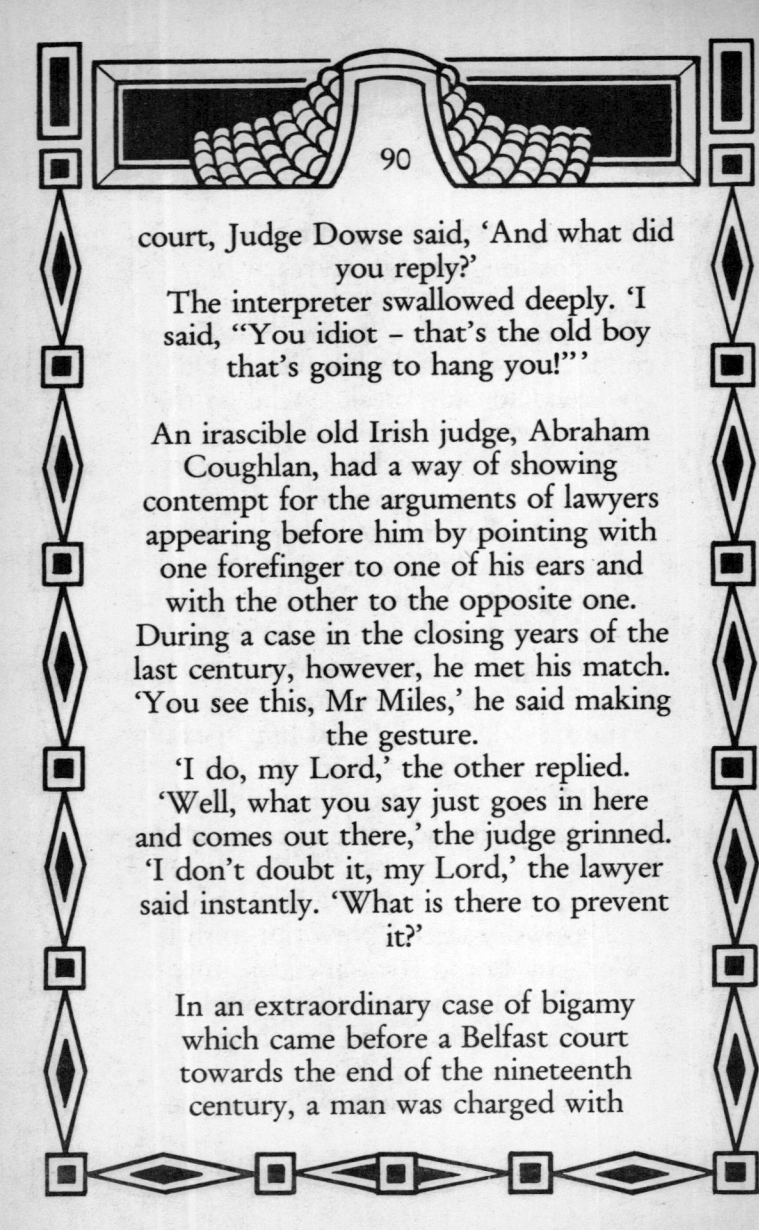

court, Judge Dowse said, 'And what did you reply?'

The interpreter swallowed deeply. 'I said, "You idiot – that's the old boy that's going to hang you!"'

An irascible old Irish judge, Abraham Coughlan, had a way of showing contempt for the arguments of lawyers appearing before him by pointing with one forefinger to one of his ears and with the other to the opposite one. During a case in the closing years of the last century, however, he met his match. 'You see this, Mr Miles,' he said making the gesture.

'I do, my Lord,' the other replied.

'Well, what you say just goes in here and comes out there,' the judge grinned.

'I don't doubt it, my Lord,' the lawyer said instantly. 'What is there to prevent it?'

In an extraordinary case of bigamy which came before a Belfast court towards the end of the nineteenth century, a man was charged with

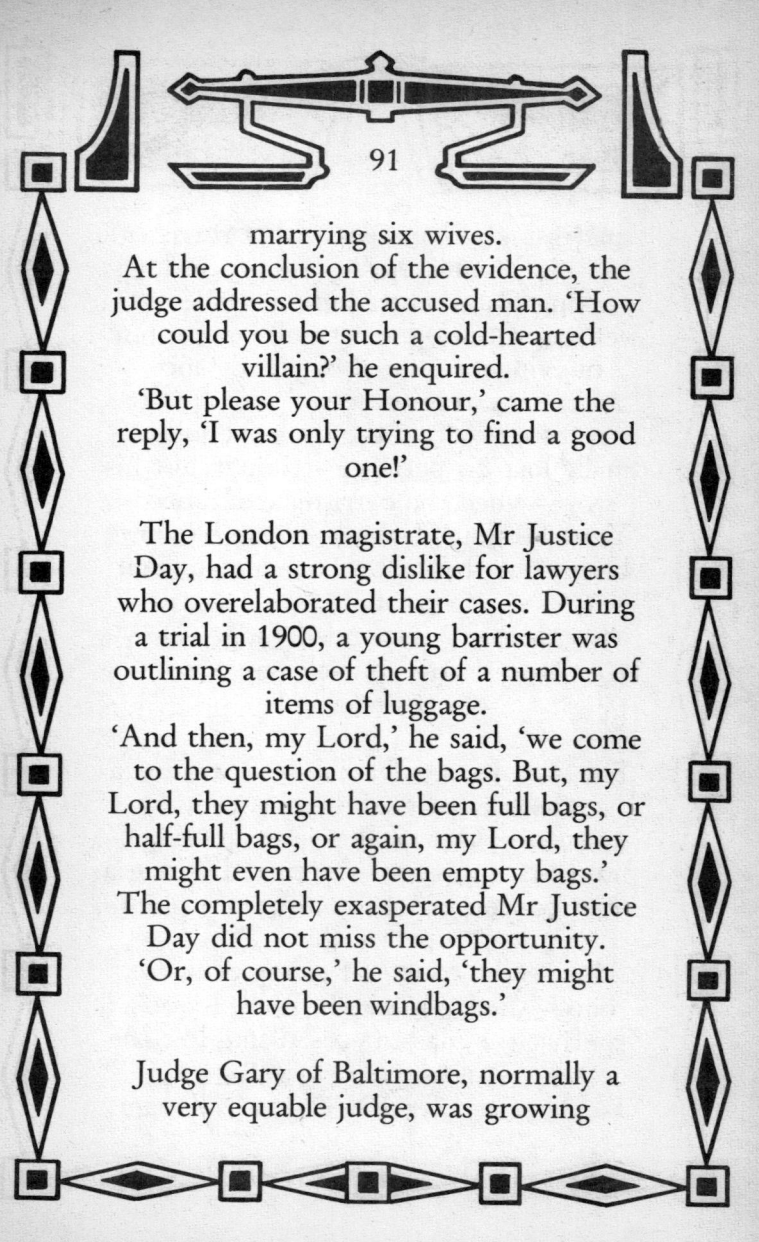

marrying six wives.

At the conclusion of the evidence, the judge addressed the accused man. 'How could you be such a cold-hearted villain?' he enquired.

'But please your Honour,' came the reply, 'I was only trying to find a good one!'

The London magistrate, Mr Justice Day, had a strong dislike for lawyers who overelaborated their cases. During a trial in 1900, a young barrister was outlining a case of theft of a number of items of luggage.

'And then, my Lord,' he said, 'we come to the question of the bags. But, my Lord, they might have been full bags, or half-full bags, or again, my Lord, they might even have been empty bags.'

The completely exasperated Mr Justice Day did not miss the opportunity.

'Or, of course,' he said, 'they might have been windbags.'

Judge Gary of Baltimore, normally a very equable judge, was growing increasingly impatient with a barrister constantly interrupting the proceedings taking place before him, in 1901 – as well as protesting at virtually every item of evidence offered by the defence.

After several unsuccessful attempts to restore order to the trial, the judge finally lost his patience – though not his wit – when the barrister exclaimed: 'Your Honour, I would rather blow my brains out than allow such a statement to stand.'

'My dear sir,' responded Judge Gary, 'you flatter yourself on your marksmanship!'

The wit of Lord Darling was famous in the later years of the nineteenth century. One of the most amusing moments in his career occurred during a case concerning the competence of an opera singer.

During the course of giving evidence, one witness remarked, 'Well, I won't say that the plaintiff could sing like the Archangel Gabriel!'

To this the defending counsel, Thomas

Duke KC, instantly responded, 'I have never heard the Archangel Gabriel.' 'Well, Mr Duke,' came the voice of Lord Darling from on high, 'that is a pleasure still in store for you!'

Thomas Roberts was facing a charge of being drunk and disorderly at Willesden Magistrates' Court in 1902. In his defence he said he was always meeting friends who insisted on buying him drinks.
'But if you are not strong enough to resist,' said the magistrate, 'you should keep out of their way.'
'Unfortunately, sir,' Roberts replied, 'I have rather bad eyesight and they see me before I see them!'

Judge James Avory was summing up a case in a London court in the early years of this century.
'Let me see,' he said to the prisoner in the box, 'you have been convicted before, haven't you?'
'Yes, sir,' replied the man, 'but it was due to the incapacity of my counsel

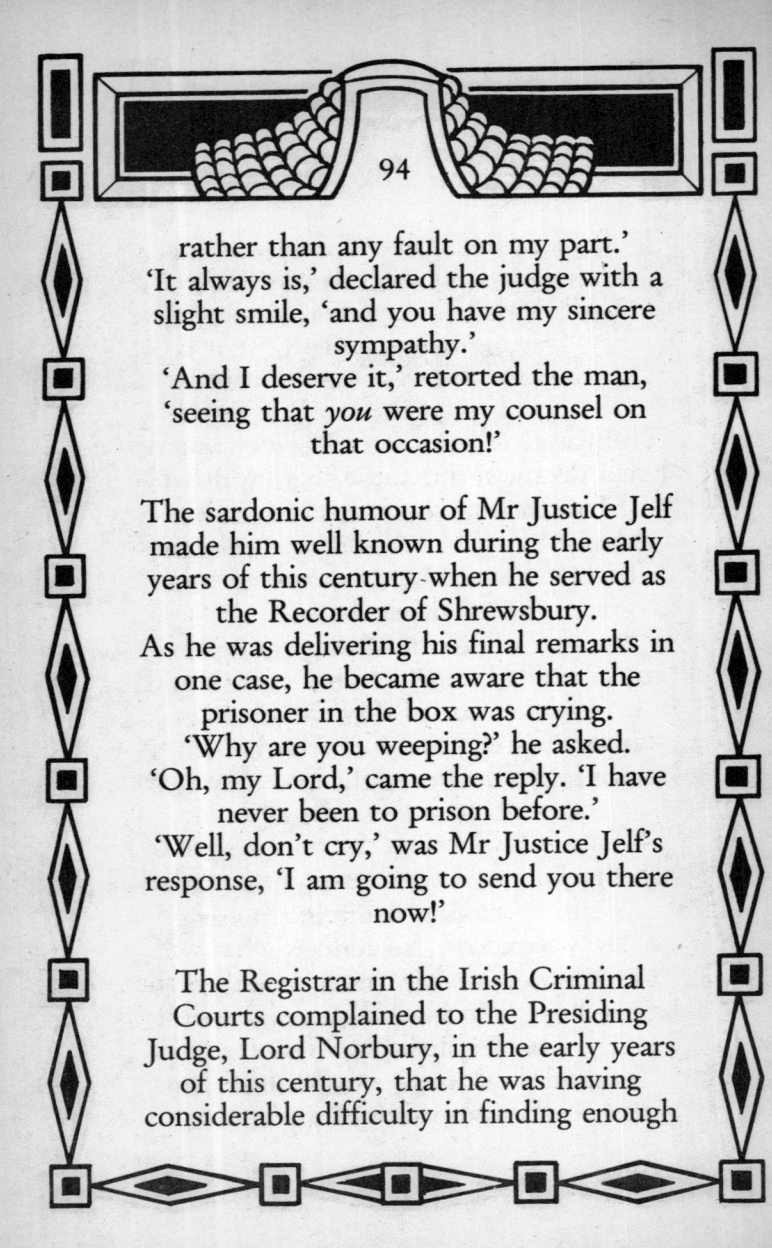

rather than any fault on my part.'
'It always is,' declared the judge with a
slight smile, 'and you have my sincere
sympathy.'
'And I deserve it,' retorted the man,
'seeing that *you* were my counsel on
that occasion!'

The sardonic humour of Mr Justice Jelf
made him well known during the early
years of this century when he served as
the Recorder of Shrewsbury.
As he was delivering his final remarks in
one case, he became aware that the
prisoner in the box was crying.
'Why are you weeping?' he asked.
'Oh, my Lord,' came the reply. 'I have
never been to prison before.'
'Well, don't cry,' was Mr Justice Jelf's
response, 'I am going to send you there
now!'

The Registrar in the Irish Criminal
Courts complained to the Presiding
Judge, Lord Norbury, in the early years
of this century, that he was having
considerable difficulty in finding enough

copies of the New Testament for witnesses to use when being sworn in. 'They are continually stealing them!' he reported angrily.

'Never mind,' replied Lord Norbury, 'if the rascals read the book it will do them more good than the petty larceny will do them mischief. However, hang the book in chains in future, and perhaps that, by reminding the fellows of the fate of their fathers and grandfathers, will make them behave themselves!'

A little ten-year-old girl came into the witness box before Sir John Ross, the judge in a Dublin court. Before she gave her evidence, the kindly old man impressed upon her the importance of telling the truth whatever anyone else might have said.

'Do you know,' he added, 'what will happen to you after you have taken the oath if you say anything that is untrue?'

'Oh, yes, sir,' the little girl said almost breathlessly, 'I will not be given any witnesses' expenses!'

During a court case in Melbourne, in 1909, which resulted from a drunken brawl in a bar, one of the convicted men insisted that he better than anyone knew when he was drunk. When asked by the magistrate to explain this claim, the man replied:

'I go on drinking till I think I'm drunk. Then I drink more till I believe I am sober. Then I am sure that I am drunk!'

Judge Michael Kerr of Swansea had a passionate hatred of the giving of credit by traders, and frequently made mention of this in court. In 1909, he was trying a case where a milkman was endeavouring to recover £13 for milk supplied to a customer.

Addressing the man, Judge Kerr said, 'But I thought everyone paid for their pennyworth of milk each day it was delivered?'

'Oh no, your Honour,' said the milkman, 'quite a lot don't. I have served your Honour's house with milk and have not been paid for two months.'

At this the judge paused a moment, and then said: 'Well, you will not supply me any more. You will be watering my milk to make up for this £13 you are going to lose!'

A man named Lewis was defending himself against a charge of wounding with intent before Baron Parke at Leicester Assizes, in 1909. The main thrust of his defence was that he was a peaceable man by nature.

'My Lord, I've been called a quarrelsome man,' he said in the full flow of his argument, 'but that's a downright falsity. For, look here, how can I be a quarrelsome man when I've been bound over twenty-three times to keep the peace?'

A soldier named Cracker Johnson appeared before the Metropolitan Magistrate of London, Sir Henry Curtis, in 1910, charged with fighting. 'I'm sorry to see you here again,' said Sir Henry, 'for I take a great interest in you. I've known you ever since you were a boy, and, as you know, your

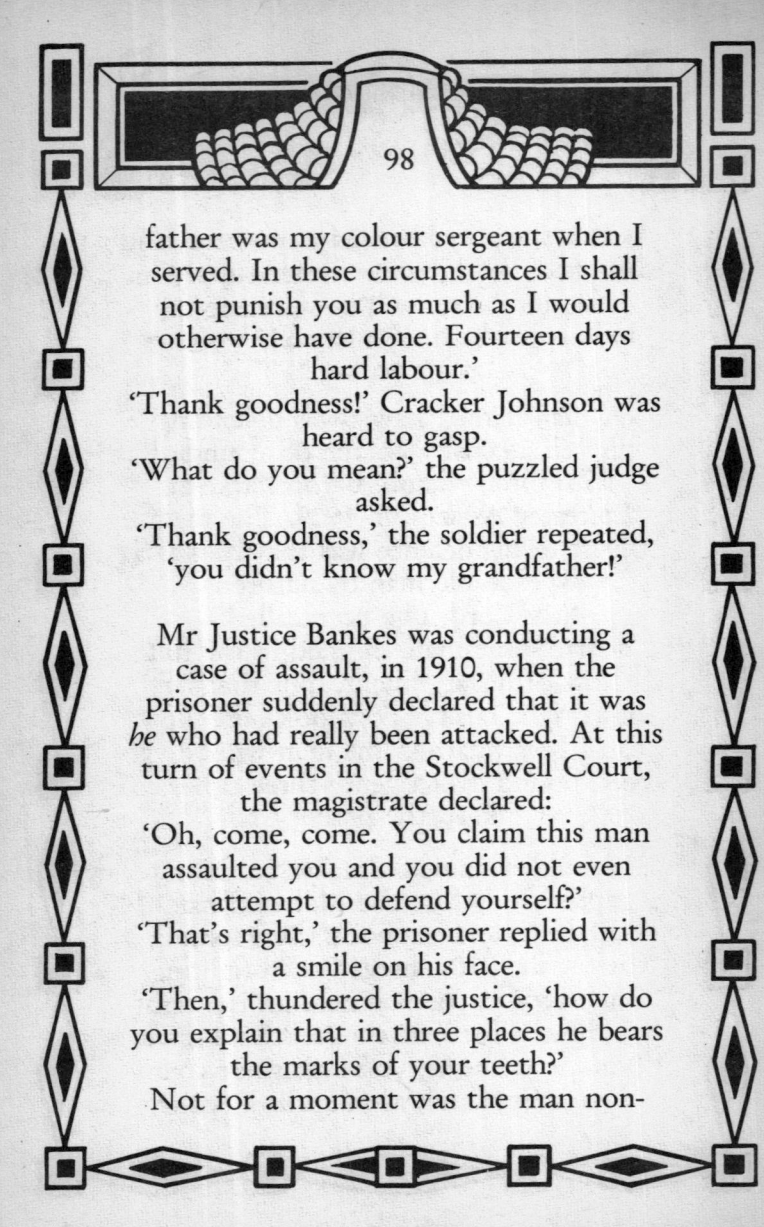

father was my colour sergeant when I served. In these circumstances I shall not punish you as much as I would otherwise have done. Fourteen days hard labour.'

'Thank goodness!' Cracker Johnson was heard to gasp.

'What do you mean?' the puzzled judge asked.

'Thank goodness,' the soldier repeated, 'you didn't know my grandfather!'

Mr Justice Bankes was conducting a case of assault, in 1910, when the prisoner suddenly declared that it was *he* who had really been attacked. At this turn of events in the Stockwell Court, the magistrate declared:

'Oh, come, come. You claim this man assaulted you and you did not even attempt to defend yourself?'

'That's right,' the prisoner replied with a smile on his face.

'Then,' thundered the justice, 'how do you explain that in three places he bears the marks of your teeth?'

Not for a moment was the man nonplussed. 'Why, he hurt me so much when he was pounding me that I had to have something to bite on so I could stand it!'

A small boy was appearing before the Children's Court in Macon, Georgia, in 1914, charged for the fifth time with stealing chickens. Judge Orvill Wallace listened to the evidence and then spoke to the boy's father who was also in court.

'This boy of yours,' he said, 'has been up in court so many times for stealing chickens that I'm sick of seeing him here!'

'I don't blame you, judge,' the father replied. 'I'm sick of seeing him here, too.'

'Then why don't you teach him how to act?' said Judge Wallace. 'Show him the right way, and he won't keep coming here.'

'Oh, I have tried to show him the right way, your Honour,' the father went on, 'but somehow he keeps getting caught coming away with the chickens!'

Another lad, Willie Henderson, was up before the Glasgow Magistrates just before the First World War charged with stealing a clock from a doctor's surgery. Having heard the evidence, the justice asked the boy why he had committed the crime.

'Well, your Honour,' he said, 'I had a bit of a pain in my side, and my mother told me to go to the doctor's to get something for it.'

'Oh, yes,' said the magistrate, nodding his head, 'but she surely didn't tell you to go and take an eight-day clock?'

A smile crossed the boy's face and he replied, 'Well, there's an old proverb that says "Time and the doctor cure a disease" and so I thought ...'

Because of a pile up of cases in the Belfast court just before the First World War, a leading judge decided to sit on Good Friday. Despite the protests from the barristers who would have to attend, the man declared, 'Better the day, better the deed.'

To this one of the complaining counsel

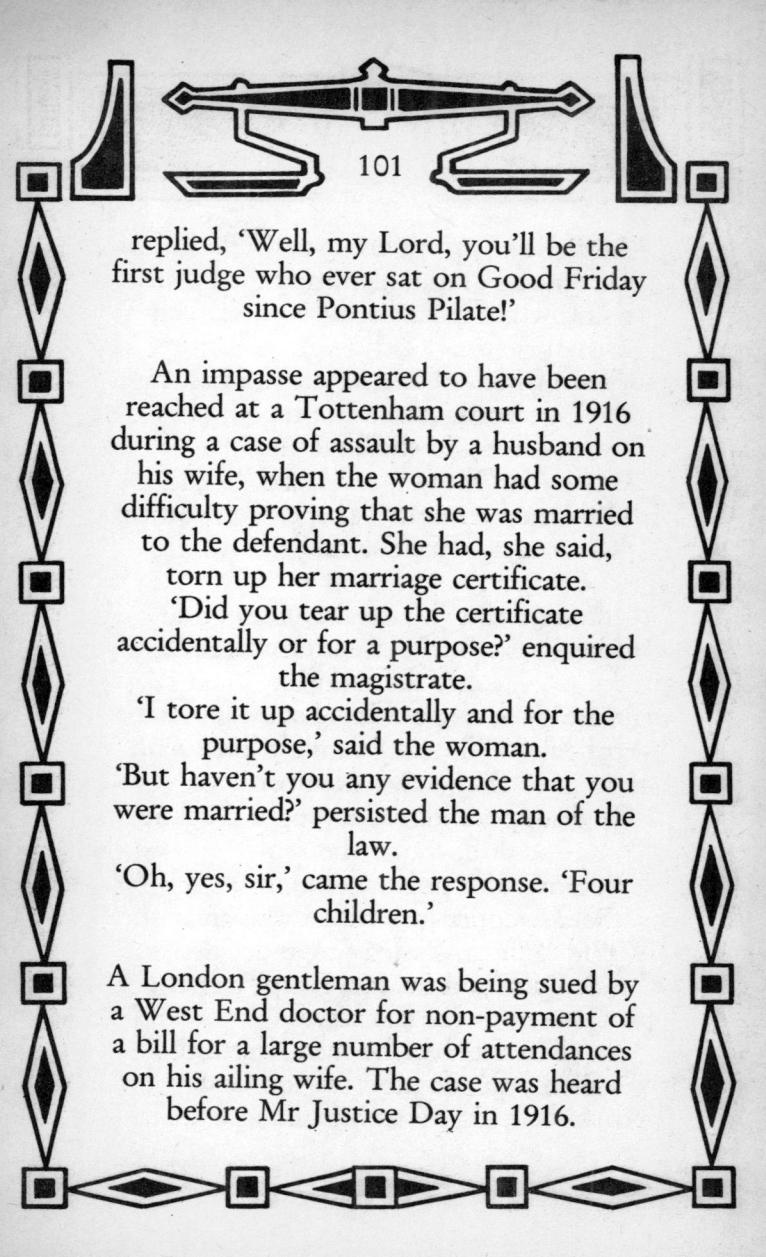

replied, 'Well, my Lord, you'll be the first judge who ever sat on Good Friday since Pontius Pilate!'

An impasse appeared to have been reached at a Tottenham court in 1916 during a case of assault by a husband on his wife, when the woman had some difficulty proving that she was married to the defendant. She had, she said, torn up her marriage certificate.

'Did you tear up the certificate accidentally or for a purpose?' enquired the magistrate.

'I tore it up accidentally and for the purpose,' said the woman.

'But haven't you any evidence that you were married?' persisted the man of the law.

'Oh, yes, sir,' came the response. 'Four children.'

A London gentleman was being sued by a West End doctor for non-payment of a bill for a large number of attendances on his ailing wife. The case was heard before Mr Justice Day in 1916.

At the end of the cross-examination of the doctor, the judge interposed to ask: 'How many times did you see this lady?'

'Two hundred and seventy times, my Lord,' came the reply.

'Is she alive?'

'Oh, yes, my Lord.'

'Dear me,' remarked the judge, 'you do surprise me!'

Magistrate Walter Matthews was addressing a burly labourer charged with assault, in 1916.

'Now, Jack, I wouldn't have expected a big fellow like you to hit a little man such as the plaintiff.'

'But suppose he called you a Cockney slob,' came the reply.

'I'm not a Cockney.'

'Well, suppose he called you an Irish slob?'

'But I'm not an Irishman,' said the magistrate.

'Well,' said the labourer, 'suppose he called you the kind of slob that you are?'

A rather pompous and self-satisfied doctor was appearing as a witness before Mr Justice Temple, in 1917, in a case of theft. The prisoner was charged with stealing items from a number of premises in Middlesex, and the doctor was appearing in his defence.

'It is my opinion,' the GP volunteered, 'that the accused is suffering from kleptomania.' And he added with a meaningful look at Mr Justice Temple, 'Your Lordship, of course, knows what that is.'

'Yes,' replied the judge without rising to the implied insult, 'it is what I am sent here to cure.'

Before his rise to prominence as a High Court Judge, Sir Samuel Evans served for a number of years as a magistrate in Glamorgan. In 1918, he presided at the case of a man charged with stealing a pair of trousers.

At the end of the proceedings, the man was found not guilty of the charge and told to go free. However, for some time he would not move from the witness box.

Anxious to get on with the next case, Sir Samuel again indicated that the man should leave.

'If you please, sir,' the fellow whispered. 'I did not like to move till the witnesses had left the court. You see I've got on the trousers that I stole!'

A Welsh magistrate was addressing a vagrant brought before him in a Cardiff court, in 1919, charged with begging.

'Are you married?' the JP enquired.

'I'm not,' the man replied, 'but my wife is.'

Angered by this, the magistrate reprimanded the prisoner. 'Don't waste our time with your miserable wit, my man,' he said. 'Remember, you must show respect to the court.'

'Upon my word I was not trying to be witty, your Honour,' the beggar went on. 'I was married, but I am separated. My wife married again – I did not. Therefore I am not married, but my wife is!'

Barrister F. E. Lockwood was

conducting a case of robbery in Lincolnshire, in the 1920s, when he called a farm labourer to give evidence about the locality in which the crime had occurred.

'What is the distance between the two places we are discussing?' he asked.

'About ten miles,' was the reply.

'Oh, you mean by road,' said Mr Lockwood, 'but how far is it as the crow flies?'

'I don't know,' said the labourer, scratching his head, 'I've never been a crow!'

A London magistrate was cross-examining a woman whose husband was in the dock accused of beating and ill-treating her, as well as having bitten off a portion of her ear. During the course of the trial, which took place in 1924, it became evident that the wife was doing her best to protect her husband.

'Isn't it true that your husband has been treating you very badly?' the magistrate asked consolingly.

'Oh, no, your worship,' was the reply.

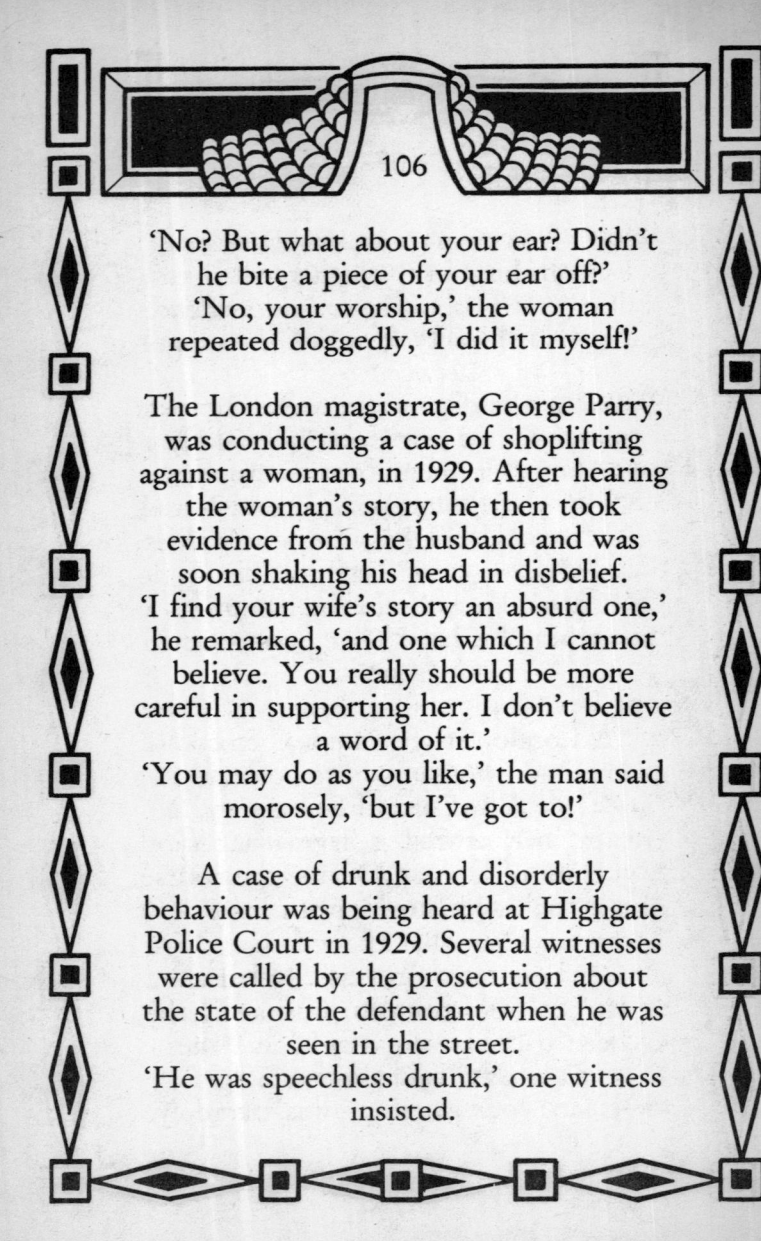

'No? But what about your ear? Didn't
he bite a piece of your ear off?'
'No, your worship,' the woman
repeated doggedly, 'I did it myself!'

The London magistrate, George Parry,
was conducting a case of shoplifting
against a woman, in 1929. After hearing
the woman's story, he then took
evidence from the husband and was
soon shaking his head in disbelief.
'I find your wife's story an absurd one,'
he remarked, 'and one which I cannot
believe. You really should be more
careful in supporting her. I don't believe
a word of it.'
'You may do as you like,' the man said
morosely, 'but I've got to!'

A case of drunk and disorderly
behaviour was being heard at Highgate
Police Court in 1929. Several witnesses
were called by the prosecution about
the state of the defendant when he was
seen in the street.
'He was speechless drunk,' one witness
insisted.

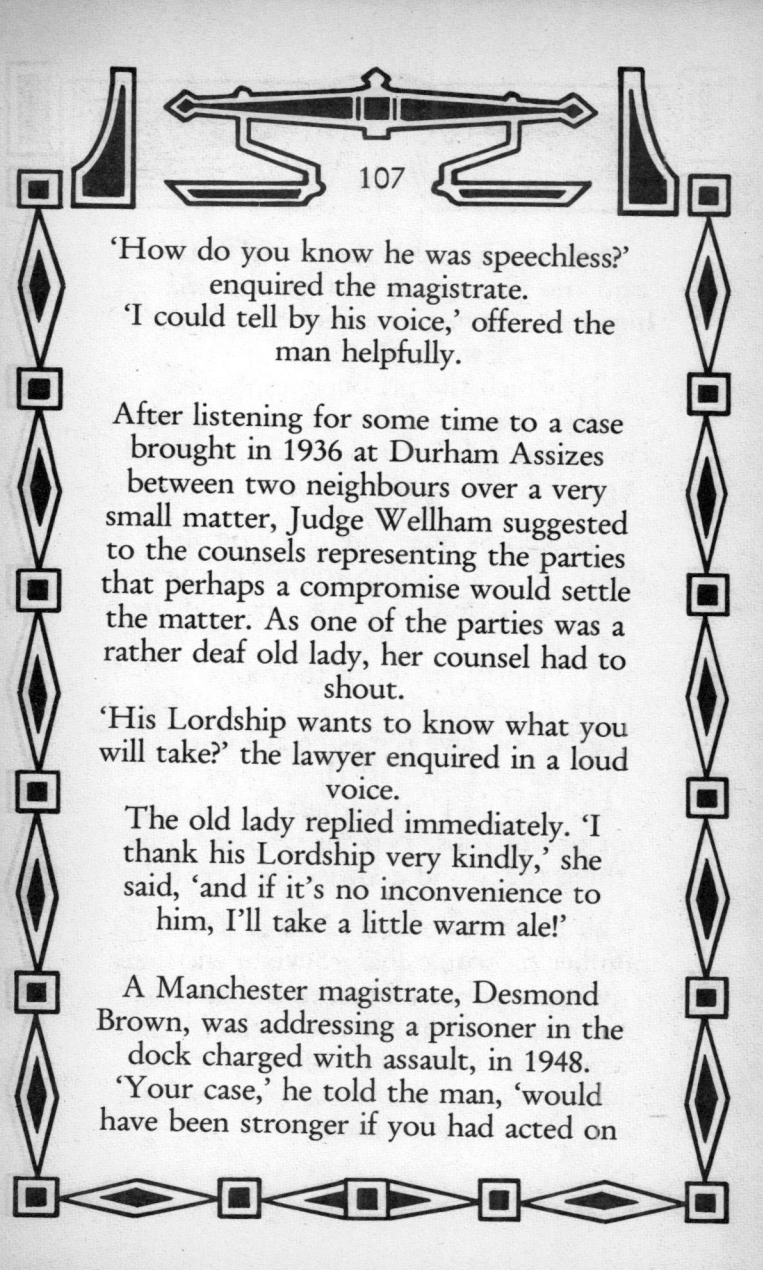

'How do you know he was speechless?' enquired the magistrate.

'I could tell by his voice,' offered the man helpfully.

After listening for some time to a case brought in 1936 at Durham Assizes between two neighbours over a very small matter, Judge Wellham suggested to the counsels representing the parties that perhaps a compromise would settle the matter. As one of the parties was a rather deaf old lady, her counsel had to shout.

'His Lordship wants to know what you will take?' the lawyer enquired in a loud voice.

The old lady replied immediately. 'I thank his Lordship very kindly,' she said, 'and if it's no inconvenience to him, I'll take a little warm ale!'

A Manchester magistrate, Desmond Brown, was addressing a prisoner in the dock charged with assault, in 1948.

'Your case,' he told the man, 'would have been stronger if you had acted on the defensive. But according to the evidence you struck first. If you had let him strike first, you would have had the law on your side.'

To which the prisoner responded swiftly, 'Yes, sir, I should have had the law on my side – but I should have had Ryan on my stomach!'

A judge was questioning a woman in the dock in a London court some years ago and proceeded to ask how old she was.

'Thirty, sir,' came the reply.

'Thirty!' exclaimed the old man. 'I have heard you give the same age in this court for the last three years.'

'Ah, yes,' said the witness, 'but I am not one of those persons who says one thing today and another tomorrow!'

A London court had processed a number of drunk charges when the final prisoner appeared before the bench. Anxious to complete the business, the magistrate urged the police constable giving evidence in the case to be as brief as possible.

'What made you think the accused was drunk?' he asked.

'Well, your Honour,' came the helpful reply, 'he was in the middle of the road trying to pick up the white line!'

A rather pompous Somerset judge was addressing a farm labourer in a case in which the man was charged with shooting a dog.

'Did you,' he said peering over his glasses, 'shoot the dog with malice aforethought?'

'Oh, no, sir. I didn't have no mallets. I shot him with a gun.'

After quietening the laughter in the court, the somewhat red-faced justice went on. 'You don't seem to understand. I'll put it another way. Did you shoot the dog in self-defence?'

'No, sir,' the labourer answered again, 'I shot him in the tail when he jumped the fence!'

A police constable was being examined by a magistrate during a case in London which had resulted from some

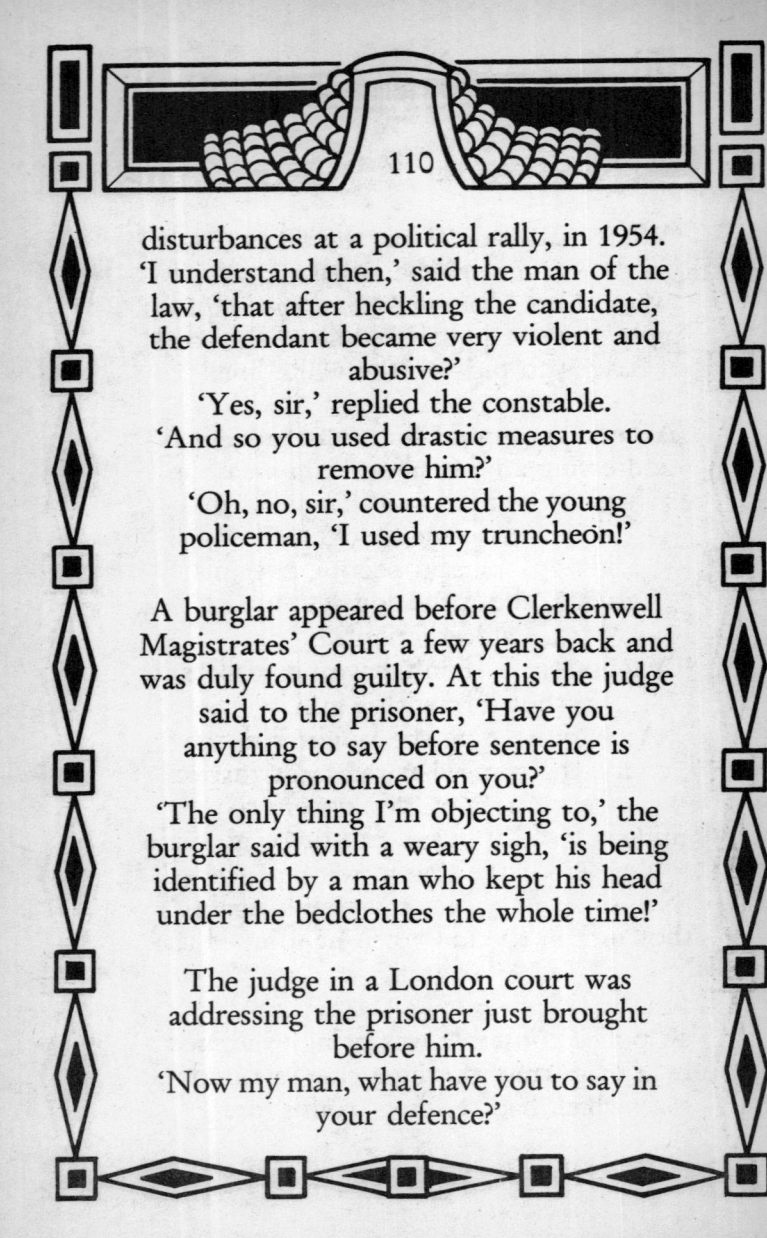

disturbances at a political rally, in 1954.
'I understand then,' said the man of the
law, 'that after heckling the candidate,
the defendant became very violent and
abusive?'
'Yes, sir,' replied the constable.
'And so you used drastic measures to
remove him?'
'Oh, no, sir,' countered the young
policeman, 'I used my truncheon!'

A burglar appeared before Clerkenwell
Magistrates' Court a few years back and
was duly found guilty. At this the judge
said to the prisoner, 'Have you
anything to say before sentence is
pronounced on you?'
'The only thing I'm objecting to,' the
burglar said with a weary sigh, 'is being
identified by a man who kept his head
under the bedclothes the whole time!'

The judge in a London court was
addressing the prisoner just brought
before him.
'Now my man, what have you to say in
your defence?'

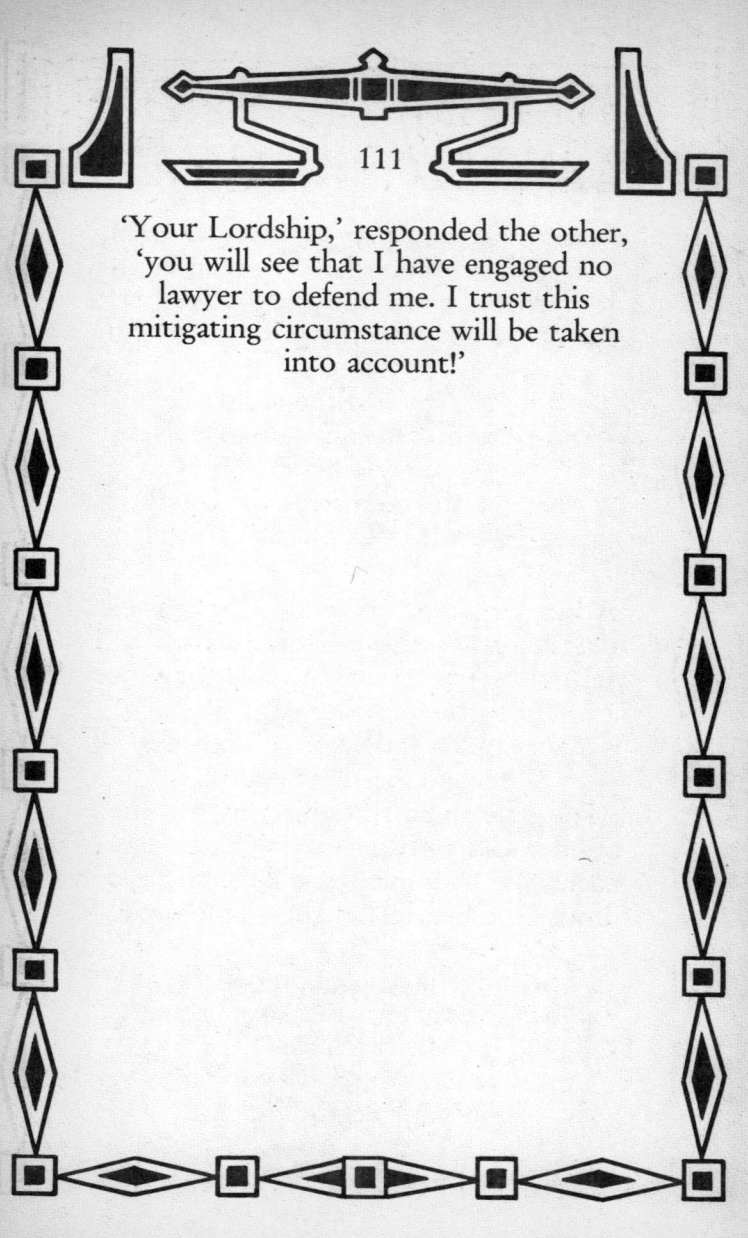

'Your Lordship,' responded the other, 'you will see that I have engaged no lawyer to defend me. I trust this mitigating circumstance will be taken into account!'